MELODY

THE
BUSINESS
OF MINISTRY

HOW TO BUILD AND SUSTAIN YOUR MINISTRY

FOREWORD BY

JOSHUA MILLS

THE BUSINESS OF MINISTRY
HOW TO BUILD AND SUSTAIN YOUR MINISTRY

Author Photo: Tiffany King | Makeup Artist: Bethany Joy Chamberlin
Cover Design & Interior Layout: www.palmtreeproductions.com
Printed in the USA

ISBN (print): 978-0-9975585-2-4

ISBN (Kindle): 978-0-9975585-3-1

Library of Congress Control Number: 2017905340

Scripture references:

Scripture taken from the HOLY BIBLE, NEW INTERNATIONAL VERSION ® is marked NIV. Copyright © 1973, 1978, 1984 Biblica. Used by permission of Zondervan. All rights reserved.

Scripture taken from The Message is marked MSG. Copyright © 1993, 1994, 1995, 1996, 2000, 2001, 2002. Used by permission of NavPress Publishing Group.

Scripture taking from The Living Bible is marked TLB. The Living Bible copyright © 1971 by Tyndale House Foundation. Used by permission of Tyndale House Publishers Inc., Carol Stream, Illinois 60188. All rights reserved. The Living Bible, TLB, and the The Living Bible logo are registered trademarks of Tyndale House Publishers.

To Contact the Author:

www.melodybarker.com

CONTENTS

I have learned that a person with experience can be much more effective than someone who only has a theory. Melody Baker is an anointed author with great skills, talents, and a rich heritage of practical ministerial experience. Melody has carefully crafted and fileted both the truth and facts to lay a firm and unshakable foundation of how to establish and flourish in ministry. Please read this book with the intention of applying these time-proven truths that will surely enrich your spiritual journey --- I wish I could have had a book like this 47 years ago!

DR. CLARICE FLUITT

INTERNATIONALLY RECOGNIZED CHRISTIAN LEADER AND LIFE STRATEGIST, AUTHOR OF RIDICULOUS MIRACLES

WWW.CLARICEFLUITT.COM

Melody Barker has grown up in a ministry environment, has served full time in ministry, and has interacted with many ministers and those who are starting out. Through her years of experience and observation she has gleaned wisdom that can help those who are getting started. You will be empowered through the many practical insights she reveals within *The Business of Ministry* that will encourage you to build a strong ministry from the foundations up.

PATRICIA KING

FOUNDER, PATRICIA KING MINISTRIES

WWW.PATRICIAKING.COM

Over the last several years I have seen Melody learn and walk out everything that is in this book. She has learned how to host events and create a plan of action for your ministry. She has learned what works best and what not to do. This is a tremendous book to help you in your life and ministry. You will learn how to plan and strategize; where you want to go and how to get there.

JOAN HUNTER
AUTHOR, HEALING EVANGELIST
WWW.JOANHUNTER.ORG

This book is a "must have" for all ministers! What Melody has captured in this amazing book will help launch your ministry! Not only will this book help launch your ministry, it will provide much needed structure and tools that will have a lasting impact on generations to come.

PASTOR JOHNNY ORTIZ
THE GATHERING PLACE
PORT NECHES, TEXAS

Melody Barker brings a rare and refreshing voice in her book, *The Business of Ministry.* The wisdom, practical advice, and intelligent perspective is a gift to any start-up or established ministry. In a day where God is calling many to jump into the adventure of full-time ministry this book holds invaluable tools and secrets. Coaches and experts would charge thousands, but Melody offers a true gift to the body. As a woman leading her own ministry, I can personally think of many long nights and hard days where the insight offered here would have been an answer to prayer. Saying yes to God's call on your life is step one. It's the standard of excellence that you release in your ministry that will give merit and value to that initial "yes." I highly endorse this book as a shining light in the complicated road to fulfilling God's call on your life.

ANNIE BYRNE
EXECUTIVE DIRECTOR MOMENTUM MINISTRIES
WWW.IMOMENTUM.ORG

FOREWORD BY JOSHUA MILLS

I f there's one question that we've heard time and again in the course of our travels around the world it's the question, "How do I get into the ministry?" I believe it's an honest question being asked by those who are legitimately called of God ... and yet, they're not sure how to get from the place of being called into the place of being sent. The difference is in the details.

God is into the details. If you need proof, just take a look at the world around you. Better yet, take a look at the tiniest snowflake through a microscope! All of creation is filled with the most intricate and specific designs that make up the bigger picture. Attention to the smallest details can result in the greatest rewards.

When God wanted to establish His temple in the earth He gave Solomon very specific instructions through David in order to complete this task with heavenly precision.

> "... David gave Solomon the plans for the Temple and its surroundings, including the entry room, the storerooms, the upstairs rooms, the inner rooms, and the inner sanctuary— which was the place of atonement. David also gave Solomon all the plans he had in mind for the courtyards of the Lord's Temple, the outside rooms, the treasuries, and the rooms for the gifts dedicated to the Lord. The king also

gave Solomon the instructions concerning the work of the various divisions of priests and Levites in the Temple of the Lord. And he gave specifications for the items in the Temple that were to be used for worship."

1 Chronicles 28:11-13 NLT

In this book, Melody Barker skillfully and accurately compares the building of a ministry to the building of a house. The Word of God declares that on this side of the cross, the Holy Spirit indwells the believer, and corporately together we have become the temple where His Glory resides.

"Don't you realize that all of you together are the temple of God and that the Spirit of God lives in you?"

1 Corinthians 3:16 NLT

Just as Solomon received instruction for the temple, I believe God desires to reveal Himself to each and every minister of Christ today. He desires to bring divine insight and guided revelation to those called to ministry so they can minister more effectively in establishing God's kingdom on the earth.

In the early days of our ministry, Janet and I had many mentors who would speak into our lives and help us navigate the path the Lord had placed in front of us through the books that they had written. One of the most beneficial tools we had in our hands during those days was a simple minister's handbook filled with godly wisdom, advice, and practical instructions for presenting our ministry with integrity and properly stewarding the anointing in a way that would glorify God. Well, that was twenty years ago and that book has since become outdated, so many things have changed over the years. Technology has changed. Conferences have changed. Church planting has changed. Ministry has changed. But the ways of God have never changed and for that reason I'm so thankful that Melody has been led by the Lord to create a resource that is desperately needed within ministry circles today.

I highly recommend and appreciate the ministry of Melody Barker. Coming from an exceptional legacy and family of world-class ministers, Melody has both the anointing and the insight to write this book. It is a modern handbook for the modern ministry. Filled with concise and accurate understanding of how to prepare, establish, and build a ministry that will both glorify God and enable you to succeed in the call that is upon your life. This book is filled with details that make a difference. This book is a blueprint for building the ministry that God has appointed for you!

JOSHUA MILLS
INTERNATIONAL GLORY INC.
PALM SPRINGS, CA / LONDON, CANADA
WWW.JOSHUAMILLS.COM

AUTHOR'S NOTE

As I sit down to write this book I am thinking about you, the reader. I want this to be so much more than a book you put on your shelf to go with all the other books on your shelf. If you're reading a digital copy, I do not want this to be something that you agree is a great resource, but leave in the cloud.

I want to impress upon you—almost with a sense of urgency— the importance and precaution for which you'll be using this resource. Everything that you do and will do in this life is built on the foundation of who you are and what you believe. If you want greatness, if you want to stand out or stand above, or if you want to stand strong, you are going to have to go deep, to the very core of you are.

What do I mean when I write "who you are"? I mean, your belief system. Your values. Your perception. Your past. Your relationships. Your knowledge. Your life choices. Plus, in the middle of getting down to who you are, you will need to bring God into every area of who you are too.

Every word written in this book is here to encourage you to pursue and be a participant in God's plan for your life. Love the Lord with your whole heart. Increase your knowledge of Biblical truths and principles. Hold fast to His words and let everything you desire in life be built on a strong foundation of faith, trust, hope and love in God. Let your foundation be so strong that you will withstand any attack from your enemies. Use your faith to create a level of determination and put forth every effort to succeed in your life, love and ministry.

I believe everything is possible! It is who I am. If your desire is to have a thriving and expanding ministry, I believe you can do it. I will share with you my experiences, development opportunities and strategy for building. I believe this will help you identify and outline the purpose and growth for yourself as well as for your ministry.

Building a ministry is like building a house. A strong and well-maintained foundation is monumental to sustaining the ministry. The spiritual covering is just as important as the physical roof. Structure for the house comes from the walls and for a ministry the partners and volunteers provide the same structural support. God is your contractor and this book is the start of your blueprints.

Through this book, I am going to share with you what I consider to be the most vital information for your ministry. It is all about how you want to do it and how God has created you to do it. This book is not the only way to start a ministry but it is based on real experiences and harsh learning curves. Consider this book a thought-provoking outline that will help you further discover more and more of God's plan and purpose for your ministry specifically. However, because you will have taken the time to answer the questions and read the information, I do strongly believe, when you get to the last page you will be confident and know what your next steps are to building and sustaining your ministry.

CHAPTER ONE

BUILDING YOUR HOUSE

Starting a ministry is like building a house. It requires attention to detail and intentional planning. The process can be time consuming, expensive and at times, it can be boring. There are rules, regulations, and requirements that factor in long before you get to pick the color of the paint and the plants out front. There are a hundred different programs on television that will show you how to flip or remodel a house. Have you noticed how few, if any, shows tell you how to build a house?

WHY IS THAT?

Building a house correctly with the proper time necessary, plus making it television-worthy, would be a difficult and nearly impossible task. There are too many details to cover in a forty-five-minute show. Even the tiny houses can barely make it into an episode.

HOW DOES THIS APPLY TO YOU AND YOUR MINISTRY?

As of 2015, there are more than 1.5 million non-profit organizations in the United States. We're going to focus on what makes your ministry stand out among the crowds. You'll learn how to show donors that your organization is not only worth looking at but it's worth supporting as it grows.

For some, full time ministry is a calling and my goal is to make this book a resource that gives you the tools to build a strong ministry. For others, this book will become a guide to help others gain structural insight or expand their ministry.

It is important to understand that this is written for each ministry to use as a resource to aid in the fulfillment of what God has called the ministry to accomplish. God gives plans and purpose to our lives. I completely believe that we must do our part in participation with God's plans for our lives and ministry to truly accomplish our full potential.

When I write, or refer to how to "build your ministry" it is so that you have practical knowledge to go hand in hand with the Holy Spirit led inspiration for your ministry. Together, we are going to look at the correlation of building a house with building your ministry. We're going to look at each layer of structure and support just as a contractor would oversee every aspect of construction.

Avoid getting in over your head by applying qualified strategy in combination with God's calling and anointing on your life. At some point, you will feel like you are unqualified to build or maintain your ministry but God is faithful to honor and protect His word.

> Then the word of the Lord came to Solomon, saying: "Concerning this temple which you are building, if you walk in My statutes, execute My judgments, keep all My commandments, and walk in them, then I will perform My word with you, which I spoke to your father David. And I will dwell among the children of Israel, and will not forsake My people Israel."
>
> 1 Kings 6:11-13 NKJV

ALL PLANS SHOULD START WITH BLUEPRINTS

The blueprints for your ministry come in the form of clearly defining the vision and the mission for your ministry. Identifying what you believe and discovering your core values will help you define the vision of your ministry. It will help you as well as others understand why your ministry does what it does and reaches who it reaches. After accepting the call into ministry, your vision statement should be the first thing you invest your time into.

You will want to do ministry and start designing, but I want to encourage you to buckle down and focus on these foundational elements before you start to build. Identifying what you do, what your purpose is and who you want to help will not only make you more effective in doing that, but it will also help you steer clear of opportunities that are not in alignment with the goals or focus of your ministry.

MONEY SAVER TIP

Building without a clearly defined vision or mission statement will cause more expensive redesign or restructuring.

I had a friend who was an architect. He was drawing out plans for a family that was wanting to add on a room to their house. He listened to what they envisioned for the house. He paid close attention to details and did he did his best to draw on paper what they saw in their heads. When it came time to show the couple the blueprints, he went over each area of the new room and what features it would have. The couple made comments and made changes to the drawing. When he was telling me about the changes he was making to the blueprints I asked him how hard it was to make those changes. He said quickly, "So much easier to change the location of a wall on paper than after the wall has been built." When it came time to build, the contractor ordered all the supplies. The crew placed the stakes in the ground and construction began. As the room was finished and they removed the original wall to open to the new space, both my friend and his clients were thrilled with the new room!

The layout and drawing needed minor adjustments to meet the needs and expectations of the clients. This can happen in ministry, but it's best if it happens early on. Once your ministry is established with a mission you will have gained support and momentum for that cause. When you change the focus of your ministry, you then must get your supporters on board with the change or find all new support.

At this point you might be thinking, what is the difference between a vision statement and a mission statement. I have found in Laurie Beth Jones' book *The Path: Creating Your Mission Statement for Work and for Life* the definition that brings clarity and distinction to the two words:

DEFINITIONS

 **MISSION** *is defined as a specific task that a person or group is sent to perform. Having a personal mission statement helps you to focus on what God has called you to be and do.*

VISION *can be defined as looking into the future and visualizing the results that you anticipate happening as a result of your mission and the plan of action that is implemented. Developing a personal mission statement is the first step in identifying/clarifying what God has called you to do. This becomes the basis for formulating your ministry plan.*

In this book, Laurie also gives an outline for writing a personal and professional mission statements. I appreciate her focus on creating a concise and easy to remember mission statement. Here are some risks if the mission statement is too long:

- You can't remember it
- You lack the ability to focus

- People will not be able to memorize it

- People forget it

- People lose interest

- It is not specific enough (the mission statement is including everything and not accomplishing anything)

- The "how" becomes cloudy or unclear

The Bible instructs us to take time and make the vision clear.

Then the Lord answered me and said:
"Write the vision
And make it plain on tablets,
That he may run who reads it.
For the vision is yet for an appointed time;
But at the end it will speak, and it will not lie.
Though it tarries, wait for it;
Because it will surely come,
It will not tarry."

Habakkuk 2:2-4 NKJV

After studying this concept for writing my own mission statement, I struggled with it for a couple of months. Initially, I narrowed it down but then I realized the wording I was using only led to the encouragement of others without producing a result. One night, I sat down at my desk and I told myself that I would not go to bed that night until I finalized my personal mission statement. It was that night that I clearly defined what it is that I want to do with my life.

> # My mission is to teach, coach and produce excellence in those pursuing their purpose and significance in life.

WHY DID I CHOOSE TEACH, COACH AND PRODUCE?

I love teaching! I love giving people insight or information that can change their position or outlook on particular topics. I love coaching! I love helping people identify what it is that they want to do instead of settling for where they feel they must stay. I chose to use the word "produce" because I am results oriented. I want to make sure that I am working on a project with an expected outcome. Plus, if I am working with someone, they know that they can expect results to be produced.

WHY DID I CHOOSE EXCELLENCE?

 **EXCELLENCE** *means extremely high quality.* I strive to do everything with excellence. I don't want to do something half-way or without my whole heart or enthusiasm.

WHY DID I CHOOSE PEOPLE PURSING PURPOSE?

I needed to identify who I wanted to work with. I use the word purpose with reference to Jeremiah 29:11 where God says He knows "the plan and purpose" for our lives.

WHY DID I CHOOSE PEOPLE PURSUING SIGNIFICANCE?

I like the way John C. Maxwell defines significance. He says, "Significance comes when you add value to others—and you can't have true success without significance." I identified that I wanted to work with people who not only wanted to make their own lives better, but they also want to impact and make the lives around them better too.[1]

In one well-written sentence, I can communicate what I want to do with my life. I do not trip over the words or forget part of my purpose. This is what I want you to be able to do as well. From this one sentence, I can look at any opportunity and ask myself if this is something I should say yes or no to. I can live my life on purpose and at the same time help other people identify if they should want to work with me to maximize their potential.

CAN A LACK OF VISION OR MISSION STATEMENT CAUSE A MINISTRY TO FAIL?

It has been said that, "If you don't know where you're going, any road will get you there." This is true, but often, not clearly defining where you want to go will mean you will not go anywhere of significance. I believe this is the same for a ministry that has not taken the time to identify its mission statement.

I think ministries can run the risk of placing all growth and success in God's hands. In doing so, they shift all responsibility to God and do not do the hard work that is required of themselves. It used to frustrate me (and honestly probably still does) when people would make comments like:

- "It's not my responsibility to build the ministry, it's God's."

- "It's up to Him to do it. Not me."

- "However God wants it done is how it will be done."

- "It's His will and not mine."

I agree that God's hand must be on a ministry to see it grow but I also firmly believe that He has not called anyone to ministry just to refuse its growth or impact. I do believe that if a ministry is struggling to grow or not growing in any area, then the ministry directors or board should evaluate the plan in place and see if it is in alignment with the mission or vision of the ministry.

If the mission is unclear the purpose is not promoted or protected. For example, I worked with a ministry that was trying to minister specifically to early college and career aged adults. It was communicated during planning meetings that the goal was to create a specific networking and relationship building opportunity for the young adults in efforts to keep this group of people engaged in church. It was not an additional worship service and it wasn't supposed to look like an additional service. The leaders developing this young adult program wanted the strength of relationships created so that as their college or career advanced, they would have strong relationships helping them maintain attendance in church, as well as, encourage their Christian faith. Three months in, the attendance had grown to forty young adults but during this time, the focus for its purpose faded. Some of its leadership shifted the focus of the group to look and feel more like a worship service and an hour-long message. At six months, the young adults group had shrunk to sixteen people and a majority was the leadership and volunteers that made the group function. At the end of six months, the young adults program was cancelled. Church leadership did not see the fruit of the financial or time investment required to keep it going. After this attempt, there have been a few promising young adult's programs arise but there have also been just as many attempts that did not work. When the mission is compromised, any support will be weakened. The group once had a great amount of support and momentum but due to the compromise for the mission it became unsustainable.

BUILD ACCOUNTABILITY FOR YOU AND FOR YOUR MINISTRY

Does it shock you or break your heart when you see a pastor has been arrested for a crime? Regardless of what the allegations are, whether they are true or false, the media gets a hold of these situations and turns them into national news. A ministry caught embezzling or caught in accusations of child abuse is like a five-car accident. Most people will slow down to watch and see how much detail they can capture as they pass by but it doesn't stop there. They will go on to talk about it and the details will change from facts to opinions. To avoid these scandals, ministries and leaders of ministries need accountability from the board members in effort to protect the potential and future of the ministry.

Looking at scripture, it could appear to be impossible to be a public representation of Jesus Christ walking on this earth. God has given us grace but we should never put ourselves in the position of relying on grace more than we rely on God. Regardless of how you live your life, as a Christian, you will be held to a higher standard of behavior and even possibly, an unreachable standard of perfection. If God has called you to ministry, then I would take a good amount of time and ask Him to show you how to live that calling. Once He has shared with you how to live that calling, then share it with those who will hold you accountable to that standard.

When my grandmother accepted Jesus as her Lord and Savior, she immediately changed to a new person. When she got the revelation that Jesus was inside her, she stopped cussing, smoking and drinking. When she received the Baptism of the Holy Spirit, God spoke to her and told her to stop painting her nails. I never saw her with nail polish on her fingers or toes. She could wear make-up and lipstick, but when she told me she couldn't wear nail polish I said, "I do not understand that."

She took a moment and said, "When I got saved, God told me to stop wearing nail polish. So, from that day to this, I have never painted my nails." She did not waiver or compromise. She lived everyday to fulfill the call of God on her life in complete obedience.

> *This is a faithful saying: If a man desires the position of a bishop, he desires a good work. A bishop then must be blameless, the husband of one wife, temperate, sober-minded, of good behavior, hospitable, able to teach; not given to wine, not violent, not greedy for money, but gentle, not quarrelsome, not covetous; one who rules his own house well, having his children in submission with all reverence (for if a man does not know how to rule his own house, how will he take care of the church of God?); not a novice, lest being puffed up with pride he fall into the same condemnation as the devil. Moreover, he must*

have a good testimony among those who are outside, lest he
fall into reproach and the snare of the devil.

I Timothy 3:1-7 NKJV

I remember being a teenager and seeing news coverage of a Priest accused of sexually abusing several children. Even now, I can see the Priest being escorted by police officers with the news banner saying "Priest Arrested After Children Come Forward with Abuse Allegations." I went from looking at the television to talking to my dad who was watching with me. I said, "I don't understand how someone in ministry could do something like that! Why on earth could someone do something like this and think that they would never get caught? How did everyone around him not know something was happening and why didn't they say something sooner to stop him?" I was so upset. It was the first time I had ever seen someone in ministry abuse their position for personal gain.

When you have nothing to hide you have nothing to fear. When you do the right things in the right way you have nothing to lose because you have nothing to fear.

Zig Ziglar

I completely agree and understand that we are all human. That fact does not excuse us from the moral code of "do unto others as you would have done to you." Consider what Jesus said to the young man,

"'You shall love the Lord your God with all your heart, with
all your soul, and with all your mind.' This is the first and

great commandment. And the second is like it: 'You shall love your neighbor as yourself.' On these two commandments hang all the Law and the Prophets."

Matthew 22:37-40 NKJV

So, then each of us shall give account of himself to God. Therefore, let us not judge one another anymore, but rather resolve this, not to put a stumbling block or a cause to fall in our brother's way.

Romans 12:12-13 NKJV

Obey those who rule over you, and be submissive, for they watch out for your souls, as those who must give account. Let them do so with joy and not with grief, for that would be unprofitable for you.

Hebrews 13:17 NKJV

My brethren, let not many of you become teachers, knowing that we shall receive a stricter judgment.

James 3:1 NKJV

Be willing to ask yourself personal questions about your relationship with the Lord. Be willing to truthfully answer where you are in you walk with the Lord, the care of your relationship, how much time you give to your relationship with the Lord. Working in ministry does not replace your need for a relationship with God. If anything, it makes you more reliant on God. It makes His voice the most valuable voice of wisdom, direction and discernment. Beyond building a ministry for people, you need to invest in yourself daily so that you have something to live on or share on daily.

I attended a leadership conference a couple of years ago and the president of the organization shared his plan for personal growth and organizational development. I took pages of notes and often refer to these notes when sharing with others who need a plan for growth. He said every day he listens to an hour of teaching on a topic that interests him. He reads one book a month in addition to his daily Bible reading and he attends one conference a year that he is not responsible for speaking at or planning. Once a month he meets with his board of advisors to give accountability for his organization. In addition to answering personal questions asked by his mentors, he is questioned regarding:

- How is his marriage?

- How are his children?

- What challenge is he facing/how can they help?

- How is his organization developing?

- Any product sales?

- Any new events booked?

- What is the financial health of the organization in comparison to the previous month?

With only four weeks between each meeting, his personal and professional life is examined and maintained. He gave his board members and mentors access to every area of his life. In addition to this group of people, he has his family and his staff to keep him accountable.

Inconsistent answers or actions would stand out to those to whom you are accountable. If you create a safety net of accountability you can protect your purpose, passion and potential. Just recently a pastor of a large church was restored to the pastoral and leadership position after a year-long sabbatical. Seeing his posts on Facebook initially brought sadness to my heart because it was an example of a church leader stumbling. Once I read the rest of the story, it made me so thankful for this pastor's honesty and humility. He shared that he had been out of the pulpit and out of ministry for a year getting sober. The stress of life along with isolating himself from others weighed on him to the point that he felt like he had to drink. The elders stepped in and removed him to protect him and the lives of all the church members. Yes, this is heartbreaking that he went through this, but thankfully he had people close enough to him to step in and aid in his restoration.

> **God showed me that He could and would replace everything that was missing in my life, but that nothing could replace Him in my life.**
>
> Zig Ziglar

MINISTRY BOARD MEMBERS AND SELECTION PROCESS

In my life and where I work, I have what John C. Maxwell has called "the inner circle." Even for my ministry team I have an inner circle of people that I look to and work with to develop ideas. Beyond brainstorming, my inner circle is a close-knit selected few that can see every aspect of my life. There are no questions they are not allowed to ask. There are no details that they are not allowed to know. They are qualified to speak to the direction of my life, evaluate my relationship with the Lord and hold me accountable for my words and actions.

For your ministry, the board should exist to protect the purpose of the ministry and the people in which the ministry encounters. To avoid a tie vote, it is best to have an odd number of people on the board. It is important that the board does not consist of all "yes" members but that the group consists of people who will say yes or no based on what is best for the ministry and not personal gain. If you select a member who is more afraid of hurting your feelings that protecting your purpose, you have selected the wrong member.

BYLAWS FOR YOUR MINISTRY

The founder, co-founder and board members for the ministry should meet and discuss the creation of your bylaws. Bylaws are your written and documented rules for the organization, the groundwork for church elections, leadership, missions, programs, and other important matters. They will identify what you believe and how you function as a ministry. Your bylaws need to be updated as needed and reviewed annually. Public legislation can affect the way a ministry can function, what laws it must follow and what requirements a ministry must meet. Any major changes in legislation can directly affect and impact the way your ministry is protected by law. Be aware of changes that are being worked or developed and as laws are passed, protect your ministry by updating your bylaws document with your board members. I highly recommend working with a company or lawyer that can help you draft and finalize your bylaws. The following questions are a good start to help you see that it sounds harder than it is. The questions are not difficult but you do need to take time with your board members to write your bylaws.[2]

Your written bylaws should answer the following questions:

- What is the focus of the ministry?

- What is the official name?

- Will there be use of DBA's (doing business as)

- How are board members elected or selected?

- How many members are on the board?

- What are the qualifications to become: President, Vice President, Treasurer, Secretary and Board Members? (You must have a President and a Treasurer)

- What are the rules for board meetings?

- How often will the board meet?

- Does the board need 100% approval to make a change in the ministry?

- What would prevent a tie?

- Can the President override the board's decision?

- What does it look like for a board member to resign?

- Under what conditions would a board member be asked to resign?

- What is the denomination of the ministry?

- What is the official statement of faith for the ministry?

- What is the official mission statement?

- What goals align with the fulfillment of the mission statement?

- Are there rules or regulations for membership (if you are starting a church)?

- What are the responsibilities of the members?

- How are staff members selected and hired?

- What are the departments of the ministry?

- What are the responsibilities of the departments?

- Does the ministry have elders?

- How are elders elected or qualified?

- What responsibilities do the elders have in leadership for the ministry?

- How are bylaws amended in response to changing legislature?

- Under what conditions would the founder, director or board members be removed from the ministry?

- What accountability is in place to prevent such circumstances from happening?

- What would cause the ministry to be dissolved?

- How would assets be dispersed if the ministry was to be dissolved?

● What is the leadership succession plan?

PREPARE TO BREAK GROUND FOR YOUR MINISTRY

God's word teaches us that to everything there is a season. Right now, you may be in the preparation season, where going into ministry is your next season. Before the season changes and you step into full-time or even part-time ministry prepare for what is coming. There are things not only in the natural but also is in the spirit that for which you need to be prepared.

> *To everything there is a season,*
>
> *a time for every purpose under heaven:*
>
> *a time to be born, and a time to die;*
>
> *a time to plant, and a time to pluck what is planted;*
>
> *a time to kill, and a time to heal;*
>
> *a time to break down, and a time to build up;*
>
> *a time to weep, and a time to laugh;*
>
> *a time to mourn, and a time to dance;*
>
> *a time to cast away stones, and a time to gather stones;*
>
> *a time to embrace, and a time to refrain from embracing;*
>
> *a time to gain, and a time to lose;*
>
> *a time to keep, and a time to throw away;*
>
> *a time to tear, and a time to sew;*
>
> *a time to keep silence, and a time to speak;*
>
> *a time to love, and a time to hate;*
>
> *a time of war, and a time of peace.*

Ecclesiastes 3:1-8 NKJV

In the natural, your ministry will need a business plan or a strategy. A mission or a vision statement is not enough to carry you through the work of the ministry. What do you want to accomplish in the first year and in the first five years? An outline with a plan of action will be needed to help you gain moral support from friends or family as well as put the plan for the mission in place.

WHAT DOES THE BIBLE SAY ABOUT PLANS?

Commit to the Lord whatever you do, and He will establish your plans.

Proverbs 16:3 NIV

May He give you the desire of your heart and make all your plans succeed.

Psalm 20:4 NIV

Suppose one of you wants to build a tower. Won't you first sit down and estimate the cost to see if you have enough money to complete it?

Luke 14:28 NIV

WHAT DOES GOD SAY ABOUT PLANS FOR YOU?

For I know the plans I have for you," declares the Lord, "plans to prosper you and not to harm you, plans to give you hope and a future.

Jeremiah 29:11 NIV

HOW HAS GOD GIVEN STRATEGIC
PLANS TO HIS PEOPLE?

I know that Jeremiah 29:11 is the easiest point to start with when giving an example of God making plans for us and we should make plans ourselves. I also firmly believe that God gives plans and does so with strategy and order. When we consider Adam and Eve in the garden, before they were created the birds of the air and fish of the seas were created. Before the birds of the air could fly and the fish of the seas could swim, He had to first create the air and the sea. Again, before He could make a home for the birds or the fish, He needed to create something out of nothing.

God created Adam and Eve because He wanted a relationship with them. He created Eve just for Adam so that Adam would not be alone. God did not create Adam and Eve and then consider their needs for a home. All of creation demonstrates God's order and strategy and it should be the same for your ministry.

> *Then God said, "Let the waters under the heavens be gathered together into one place, and let the dry land appear"; and it was so. And God called the dry land Earth, and the gathering together of the waters He called Seas. And God saw that it was good. Then God said, "Let the waters abound with an abundance of living creatures, and let birds fly above the earth across the face of the firmament of the heavens." So God created great sea creatures and every living thing that moves, with which the waters abounded, according to their kind, and every winged bird according to its kind. And God saw that it was good. And God blessed them, saying, "Be fruitful and multiply, and fill the waters in the seas,*

and let birds multiply on the earth." So the evening and the
morning were the fifth day.

Genesis 1: 9-10, 20-23 NKJV

"Strategic planning is not only a biblical concept; it is a biblical mandate. It is God's chosen method of working to establish how you and your ministry intend to carry out the Great Commission. Don't just repeat last year. Be intentional in getting God's heart and knowing how you will accomplish His mission in your setting."[3]

WHY IS STRATEGIC PLANNING IMPORTANT FOR YOUR MINISTRY?

Let me ask you this question: have you ever paid for something at the store to get home and see that you were charged twice? Or have you ever cut paper, a piece of wood, or fabric and the cut was too short leaving you with wasted material and having to buy more material because inevitably what you have remaining is not big enough to do what you needed to do?

Strategic planning is like the wise, old saying, "Measure twice, cut once." I have yet to meet a ministry that has every need met with an ample supply of consistent donor support. Everyone, whether greater or smaller, older or younger, starting out or a well-established ministry will always have needs. I have not come across a ministry with enough "extra" of anything that could or would allow doing a project and then do the same project again.

For example, if you wanted to lay a foundation for a house and ignored the physical requirements and order required to create a strong foundation, the necessary support for the structure would not be reliable or resistant to the elements. Pouring the concrete for the foundation is not the first step for the foundation. There is grading, leveling, surveying, and things like water drainage and underground cables to consider. If you pour concrete without the right elements in and around the concrete, moisture from the ground will come up through the concrete creating several problems with your foundation plus you will run the risk of ruining your carpet and furniture. Ignoring the right order will make renovating an expensive nightmare. Tearing up and pouring a new foundation is the right thing to do, but pouring the concrete correctly the first time is the best thing to do and the best use of your resources. The results of a poorly planned or strategy lacking project is not always as expensive as constructing a new foundation, but as a ministry, and as a steward of God's finances for kingdom expansion, there is no room for waste.

> *Plans fail for lack of counsel, but with many advisers they succeed.*
>
> Proverbs 15:22 NIV

PLANNING MEETINGS

When I was younger, to get things accomplished, I used my stubborn "I am always right" and "this position makes this my responsibility" attitude. I did not know or understand adding value to others, developing the strength of the team, or developing personal leadership skills. I was introduced to personal growth for leadership when I read John C. Maxwell's book *The 21 Indispensable Qualities of a Leader*. It was through his books that I understood the concept of team building and the principle "Teamwork makes the dream work." I learned leadership and team building from Maxwell; I learned about planning meetings from the service coordinator and her assistant at a fast growing, spirit-filled church. A great team with a good plan will succeed.

In short, planning meetings help the leader and the team identify the desired outcome of ministry services, fundraising, and outreach. These meetings, when used correctly will help you:

- Plan

- Solve problems

- Encourage the team

- Inspire creativity

- Give a sense of direction

- Identify the common purpose

- Help the leaders make decisions

The collective genius and creativity should always be encouraged when developing strategy for your ministry or for creating the next level of strategy. One of the greatest takeaways I received from John C. Maxwell was the importance of developing and listening to your team.

When I ask my entire team for feedback or for their ideas, I am amazed at how many great ideas they come up with. There are three people I go to when I have a plan that will affect the team. I specifically ask for their opinion on the plan and if they agree with the plan, then together, we come up with the best implementation. I discovered several years ago that most of the people I work with have a personality that needs an advanced warning for major changes. Most people do not like change much less swift change. When you're working with people who are like family, you want to show you care by considering them and their reactions when making changes. Knowing their personalities and showing that I care, I strive to have a strategic plan in place. Care for your future staff and volunteers the same way. Make a plan that will be the most beneficial and the least stressful possible for those involved.

> ## An hour of planning can save you ten hours of doing.
>
> Dale Carnegie

WHO SHOULD ATTEND A PLANNING MEETING?

The ministry director and leadership team should attend the planning meetings. This means that it will be you and those you rely on to accomplish the mission of the ministry. Any additional staff or volunteers do not need to be involved at this level. As your ministry grows, the leaders of different ministry positions can be brought in to add to the group brainstorming and planning efforts.

HOW LONG SHOULD THE PLANNING MEETING LAST?

Each meeting should have an agenda or an outline of what questions need to be asked or what area needs a solution. It's important to keep in mind that staff or volunteers will have other things they feel they need to get accomplished that day so avoid meetings that last longer than ninety minutes.

Every ministry service and conference I help to coordinate have planning meetings with our staff. Each person has a job assignment during the event and together we cover all the major aspects of our responsibility as the hosting ministry. I notice that after forty minutes, ideas start slowing down, volunteering to cover an area has slowed down and people lose excitement or anticipation for this meeting. Overall, I try to keep them short and focused because that is what works best for our team. This is an area that you will want to test and develop to see what works best for you and for your team.

> **I remember saying to my mentor, "If I had more money, I would have a better plan."**
>
> **He quickly responded, "I would suggest that if you had a better plan, you would have more money."**
>
> **You see, it's not the amount that counts; it's the plan that counts."**
>
> Jim Rohn

"Strategic plans are often the foundation for how a non-profit performs. Those with a written strategic plan tend to hold their leadership accountable for performance. They are 50% more likely to have a formal process for measuring leadership effectiveness across the organization, and to have their CEOs undergo an annual performance review. This gap is not limited to small non-profits. For those organizations without a written strategic plan, more than half do not feel that there are systems in place to ensure all stakeholders clearly share the vision and 'brand' of their non-profit. Without these systems in place, non-profits run the risk of lacking alignment between what donor's feel is important and what is actually being accomplished. Once consumers feel their contributions are being wasted, you run the risk of losing that donor now and in the future."[4]

Planning on purpose for your ministry will help you discern answers to opportunities between not right now, maybe later, and not ever. Planning prevents decision making based on an impulse or because of fear. Planning makes you prepare for opportunities you are believing God for in faith to become reality.

ENDNOTES

1. Source: http://www.success.com/article/john-maxwell-success-or-significance.

2. For sample bylaws visit: http://www.freechurchforms.com/support-files/churchbylawssample.pdf.

3. Source: http://www.christianitytoday.com/pastors/2007/july-online-only/le-031112a.html.

4. Source: http://www.forbes.com/sites/ianaltman/2016/03/20/half-of-nonprofits-are-setup-to-fail-how-about-your-favorite/#bc259cb16e6b

There are some people who live in a dream world, and there are some who face reality; and then there are those who turn one into the other.

Douglas H. Everett

CHAPTER TWO

BREAKING GROUND FOR YOUR HOUSE

Preparing to break ground for your ministry is going to be one of the most exciting phases you'll ever get to experience! Hopefully, you will only have to do this part one time. You have focused on writing the vision, making it clear, and focused specifically on what God has called you to do. You have done all the preparation. Now, let's get ready to dig deeper and look at what is needed to break ground and prepare to build.

There are three different areas that you need to consider while preparing to break ground. The first area for you to look at is your personal requirements and position. To start a non-profit ministry organization, you need to receive credentials, like ordination from a well-established ministry, school of ministry or theological seminary. This is not an area that you want to cut corners on. I would strongly encourage you to attend specific training in the area of ministry that you would like to work in. Even though it is possible to become an ordained minister through an online application process, I would highly recommend that you find alternative options for your credentials. An online application is not the best way for you to start your ministry.

WHAT IS MY RELATIONSHIP WITH GOD?

When it comes to your position, we are about to get personal. Where is your relationship with the Lord? I only ask this because you are getting ready to build a ministry and your personal faith and relationship with the Lord will be the foundation of your ministry. Your faith and tenacity will determine your ability to withstand the demands of working in full-time vocational ministry. You are about to make yourself a conduit or extension of who God is and express it to others in a greater way than you have before.

I can remember moments, even in recent history, where my faith was strong but my trust was weak. I can remember instances that have caused me to break down to my core and ask myself again, "What do I believe and who do I believe God is?" Don't get me wrong, working in full-time ministry is a blessing and it is an awesome opportunity to see God move and change lives every single day. There have been days where the prayer requests are too much, the needs are too big, and the day is too short. God is still good and He is still on the throne but there will never be a lack of need for ministry. There will never be the last request, no unread emails, or no one with a need. Ministry becomes who you are because you will live it and do it everywhere you go. Loving God and wanting to live out His purpose for your life will draw you in and fulfill you while you serve Him but you will also need to avoid the risk that comes with full-time ministry.

What risk is there in working in full-time ministry? I will quote my friend and mentor, Bobby Weber, "Do not let the work you do for God replace your relationship with God." Your personal relationship with God must always come before the business or the work of the ministry. There are days that will be too busy and a work load that will take up too much time. If you have a family, then you cannot neglect your family for the sake of your ministry.

> ## Do not let the work you do for God replace your relationship with God.
>
> **Bobby Weber**

Depending on how you manage your personal relationships, they will become the greatest source of joy or the sorest subject in your life. If they come after your work or your ministry, they will become an unnecessary sacrifice "for the sake of the call" to ministry.

Rick Renner is a Christian leader, pastor and family friend that I would consider to be one of the wisest people I know. When traveling with the ministry, we had the opportunity to go to Russia and to minister in his church in Moscow. It was amazing! This was my fourth trip and in the top two experiences I had when going to Russia. We were sitting at lunch and I asked him some business of ministry questions. One of the questions I asked was about his relationship with the Lord. His answer has stuck with me from that day to this, he said, "In the morning, I get up and I get a cup of coffee and my Bible. I spend time with the Lord every morning and do not have physical food until I have had my spiritual food."

There are several things that you can do to make sure that you keep your relationship with the Lord on track for growth and maturity. Here are a few:

- Set an appointment to meet with the Lord every day

- Start every day in prayer and thanksgiving to God

- Use a Bible reading app on your phone with scriptures pre-selected by calendar

- Read the One Year Bible

- Search out devotionals for leaders in ministry

- Have an accountability partner

- Get a mentor for your spiritual growth and maturity

- Set a sabbatical for yourself to take time off and away from ministry

- Attend conferences that you are not speaking at to be more receptive to the messages of other ministers

- Do your own spiritual check up – in the end you can't lie to yourself

For more insights, I encourage you to read the Parable of the Talents found in Matthew 25:14-30 and Luke 19:12-28.

WHERE DO I WANT TO BUILD MY MINISTRY?

The next two things you need to consider go hand in hand. Look for the location where you want to build and at the same time consider the climate of that area. These two things should be considered at the same time because the wrong climate in a good location will not produce the right results for your ministry. For example, if you desire to have a ministry that provides food and supplies to homeless people, you should consider where they are before building. If you are located in a posh or newly built shopping center, a fully stocked pantry with clean clothes, showers, and medical aid will not be as useful to those who need what you have because they live twenty-seven miles away from where you are located. Likewise, the surrounding climate of the ministry may not value what you are doing and other tenants could potentially be hostile to you or those you are trying to reach.

Here is a real-life example of a location and climate complication. Several years ago, out of necessity a ministry moved into a shopping center near where they were hoping to build. They had several retail spots in one location and in addition to the ministry, there were other stores, restaurants, a medical office and liquor store. On Sunday's, when the church would have services, there wasn't a lot going on in the shopping center. The mid-week service and arguments over parking became an issue with the nail salon and the liquor store. I remember one day, both of those owners came out of their store to yell at me for parking "too close to their entrance". Out of my lack of maturity or knowing more of the back story to their frustration I yelled back, "I was only here for five minutes and these spaces are not reserved for either of your businesses." Later that week when I was sharing this experience with someone else who worked in that shopping center, they let me know that church members had gone into both stores to tell them they were going to hell. The nail salon had a Buddha with a fruit bowl in front of it and the liquor store owner was selling liquor. After l learned the back story to their frustration it made me feel bad that I yelled at them. Telling the store owners or operators that they were going to hell was beyond hurtful to their relationship to other church members but I believe that it was even more damaging to their potential love for the Lord or possible decision to become a believer.

For this little church, the location was nearly perfect. It was just off a busy intersection. It had plenty of parking spaces. It was well-lit at night. The lease agreement had easy payments and friendly management. The location was perfect for their current size. They had outgrown meeting in the pastor's home but they were not big enough to take on renting a building or buying a building. For this church, the benefits of the location were considered but they did not consider the climate the neighbors created.

WHAT KIND OF ATMOSPHERE DO I DESIRE FOR MY MINISTRY LOCATION?

Another part of location and climate to consider is the safety or the comfort level of those coming to attend a service at your ministry. Climate and location is not the actual barometric pressure, elevation or even the physical address. These things could be areas that you want to consider further; I am wanting you to focus on the surrounding atmosphere of your ministry. Whether your guests are coming to serve, attend or receive ministry, you want to make them feel comfortable, welcome and appreciated.

Several years ago, we were scheduled to go to a ministry location in Tennessee. Long before the ministry date arrived I started hearing about the location. People were calling our ministry and asked if we understood where we were going. To us, we knew we were going to a banquet hall/conference center and the event was sponsored by the owners. The owners did not have a sponsoring church but wanted to restore life and hope to those who lived at the adjacent hotel. The conference center was in an old downtown area in this small city and the owners wanted to create positive change and kingdom impact in their neighborhood. As the event got closer we found out that we could not stay at the hotel adjacent to the conference center. The hotel on the property had several long-term residents and the area had a very high crime rate. The owners booked our hotel rooms fifteen minutes away.

As the ministry date got closer, those who supported our ministry around the conference center understood our hopes to go to that small town but they we're still calling to tell us to "be careful and really pray and ask God if we should go there." The phone calls caused some concern but after speaking with the owners of the conference center, we decided to keep the trip as planned.

While we were there, we had absolutely no issues with crime or neighborhood conflict. The trip went so well, we returned the following year to minister again. Since then the owners of the hotel and conference center have done major improvements and remodeled the hotel guest rooms. It was a beautiful time of ministry and I'm thankful that we exceeded the expectations of our host. We saw people healed and delivered. We saw several people dedicate their hearts to the Lord and we ministered to the staff of the hotel and conference center. The area that we were in did cause people concern and unfortunately some people chose not to attend because of where the conference was located. People called our ministry and said "I'd love to go when you are in the area, but I simply can't go where you will be this time."

Traveling ministries, like evangelism, need to consider the climate and location for personal safety. When you are invited to minister in an area that you are unfamiliar with or going to a country that is hosting you because they "found you on the internet," you need to exercise precaution and say yes to the invitation because you know and heard God say go. When you go for the right reason and not just because it's an invitation, the Lord will go before you and prepare your way.

A final thought when you are getting ready to break ground and you are considering your location and climate, look at the surrounding area for existing churches and ministries.

- How many churches are in the same neighborhood?

- Is there a ministry that is already reaching the people you want to reach?

- Will you be able to grow or extend outside of the current space easily?

- Will you be competing for parking spaces?

- Who has previously rented a space in the space you are looking to rent or buy?

- What is your proximity to the airport,
  hotels, restaurants and grocery stores?

- Are there schools near the location you're considering?

- Is the area booming with growth or going bust?

These questions should not be the only questions you ask yourself when considering the location, this is merely a good start.

If you are going to rent a building as part of your preparation for building or owning a building, look at the leasing history of the possible location.

- What was the average length of lease?

- What conditions led to previous tenants
  not renewing their lease?

- Is there a city code violation or noise complaint that
  could come from neighbors during worship?

- Will it be located next to a business that will have
  open office hours that could affect your ministry?
  Or could you negatively affect their business?

- How is the maintenance taken care of on the property?

When considering a location or climate, this is a good time to involve your ministry board or team. It would be good for your team or board to look over the surrounding neighborhood, local businesses, and location that you are considering. Remember, that when making decisions for your ministry, you shouldn't be doing it alone. Any major decisions should always be done with the consent of your board. Another benefit to having your ministry board consider the area with you, is they could potentially see reasons why you should or should not be located in that area.

HOW EASY IS MY MINISTRY LOCATION TO ACCESS BY OTHERS?

One of the factors to consider when building in an area that is underdeveloped or on the outskirts of the city, is the amount of time it will take participants to get to your ministry. Additional factors for you to consider would be:

- What is the average commute time from where you're currently meeting to your new location?

- Does traffic increasing or decreasing become a factor in affecting people's desire to come to your new location?

- How well-lit is the area surrounding you're building?

- Are the street signs clear? Do they make it possible for people to find where you're located?

Our ministry was once located in an office complex. We outgrew the conference space and started renting a neighboring church. Every time we would have a service or conference, we would go and set up and at the end of event we would tear it all down. We went from busting at the seams in the first space to very little attendance in our rented space. At first we thought it was because we moved. (Understand there is always a risk of losing ministry supporters or attendees when you move from one location to the next.) Then, gradually word got out that our new location had more room and we advertised that we have moved. That helped in attendance but overall it did not make a big difference. The more we researched why our numbers dropped so drastically we found out people couldn't find the new location. They said the roads signs were not easy to find or follow, nor were the roads well-lit.

Once we discovered what the problem was, we could find a solution. We created signs and before each service, the signs would be placed along the two roads that led from the original conference center to the church we were renting. The signs helped people find their way to the church. We continued to meet in that church once a month for a year. To some, it seemed we took a step backwards. They measured more space as more growth, less space as not sustaining growth. I would like you to consider the measurement in terms of stewardship. We chose temporary inconvenience with strategy in order to lower our expenses and increase our flexibility. We also looked at it as way to bless the local church.

After a year, we had the opportunity to buy a church building that was ten minutes closer to the city of Houston, closer to the hotels, grocery stores, restaurants and there was room to grow on the property.

The year we spent renting the church gave our ministry the opportunity to pay less rent than in the office park. This was a huge advantage for us. It allowed us to lower our outgo and maximize the income into substantial growth. It is important to remember, when you are working in ministry, you must balance the importance of the needs with cost and worth of the needs. We needed a space for our ministry to have monthly services. We carefully weighed the cost of continuing the conference center lease against the rented space with the church. The convenience of having everything set up all the time, having a place to meet for staff meetings, luncheons, prayer meetings, and so on, was really nice. The worth of having it available all day every day did not exceed its actual cost.

Changing your location or moving to a different climate will cause your ministry to be affected. Usually moving creates an immediate dip in attendance but over time it will balance or stabilize. Hopefully, knowing this will help you clearly identify your ideal location and climate.

Make a list of your own or ask yourself these questions:

- Where do you want to break ground?

- Are the ones you want to minister to near this location?

- Would this location enable or disable the ministry to accomplish all that God has called it to do?

- Is your personal position in a stable place where you can extend and build your ministry?

- Has your ministry gained support and can it sustain a location outside of your house, renting a hotel conference room or using a fellowship hall?

- Do you need your own location? (If you are considering evangelism or becoming a missionary, you do not have to have your own location or building. I would recommend that you start with a PO Box and keep your outgo at a minimum.)

Preparing to break ground is one of the most exciting phases of your ministry. You are getting to dive into your relationship with the Lord, create growth in your personal position and then determine the location that will best suit your ministry and those you will minister to.

Five ways to investigate a potential location:

1. Talk to the neighbors
2. Visit day, night, weekday, weekend
3. Check newspapers and local blogs
4. Get an app (to check crime)
5. Google the address

Brenda Desimone
Zillow Porchlight Blog, August 2013

CHAPTER THREE

PURCHASING GROUND FOR YOUR HOUSE

I have asked you about your relationship with God and your family and now we are going to get even more personal. I only say this because not only are we about to talk about where you are right now but we're also going talk about where your finances are too.

Take a moment and do a mental inventory of everything in your life. How does everything look and feel to you when you first think about it? When you think of your home, do you see a place that is disorganized, dusty and in desperate need of decluttering?

The reason why I'm asking you this is because how you organize your home and how you manage your home is most likely a good indicator of how you will organize and manage your ministry.

WHAT IS MY PERSONAL FINANCIAL POSITION?

Now think about your bank account, credit card balances (if any), your store credit cards, your mortgage and possible car payments. You may be thinking to yourself what does any of this have to do with my ministry or starting my ministry? Once you have filed for your non-profit organization or if you're in the process of filing, one of the next things you'll be doing is opening a corporate bank account. With your corporate bank account, you'll also be offered a corporate credit card. The offer will be made available based on your personal credit score and banking records.

When I wanted to launch my own website, and have an online store feature (to sell books, event registrations or coaching), I needed to open a corporate checking account. Before I could open the account, I had to obtain a DBA (Doing Business As) to show the bank that I was a business. I went to the County Clerk's office, filled out simple forms and paid the minor processing fee. Once I had the paperwork for the DBA, I went to the bank to open a corporate account. I did not know until I was answering questions to the banker what I would need in addition to the DBA. However, I knew enough to bring two forms of ID and my social security card.

The banker looked at me and asked if I wanted a credit card in addition to my checking and savings account. I thought about it for a second and then said yes. I asked her how a brand-new company could get a credit card and that's when I found out it would be based on my personal credit score. She asked if I knew what my credit score was and I said, "I have been working since I was in my mid-twenties. It's a 735." Her response was, "Well then, you shouldn't have a problem getting approved." Moments later, the credit application was approved, the checking and savings accounts were opened and I could launch my website.

When I have mentioned personal finances or credit scores, either while teaching or in a one-on-one session, I mention it because I want you to be prepared for the questions you will face. Not only that, but I want you to know as much as possible at the beginning so that as you grow, you grow in a healthy, well-prepared way that God continues to bless. I want you to have access to what you need when you need it. If you have the ability right now to improve your personal financial position, then do it. If you are not in the best position in your personal finances, make it a priority to get them organized. Reduce debt and start saving so that you will have start up finances available when you are ready to launch your ministry, work part-time, or lease your own ministry space.

I want you to have access to what you need when you need it.

As you are creating a better financial plan for yourself, create a savings account and start saving for the start-up costs or ministry development. Initially, your ministry will only have the money that you put into it. Once it gets going and you can receive donations, your finances will not be the only lifeline to the ministry surviving. However, you should always partner or give to your ministry. You should give to your ministry because you believe in what it's doing and what God has called you to do with the ministry. Plus, you will be able to ask others to give to it because you have set the example first.

As you build your savings and prepare for purchasing or renting a ministry location, take time to separate needs and wants. You only have a certain amount of start-up capital. It is so tempting to spend the $500-$1000 on a website and logo, but if you haven't successfully filed for your non-profit status, then that money should be applied to hiring a professional or a lawyer to help you file. We will discuss the timing of logo, website and advertising for your ministry, but this is not where you start.

God is a God of order and He has given you a specific purpose or calling to fulfill. Along with the specific purpose, He will give you the ability to know your order and process.

> *The steps of a good man are ordered by the Lord, And He delights in his way.*
>
> Psalm 37:23 NKJV

CAN I TRUST GOD WITH THE FINANCES FOR MY MINISTRY?

I want to encourage you. Where you are right now is not where you must stay! If you are worried about the cost of starting a ministry, that is okay. It is, as long as you do not stay worried. Recognize that start-up cost is a natural need but praise God for His supernatural ability to supply.

You should always trust and believe God for your finances. He knows your needs and for the needs of your ministry. It's important to decide from the beginning that you will know the needs, believe by faith for them, and then be a great steward of your resources.

This is how it is to be done: Every creditor shall cancel any loan they have made to a fellow Israelite. They shall not require payment from anyone among their own people, because the Lord's time for canceling debts has been proclaimed.

Deuteronomy 15:2 NIV

Be anxious for nothing, but in everything by prayer and supplication, with thanksgiving, let your requests be made known to God; and the peace of God, which surpasses all understanding, will guard your hearts and minds through Christ Jesus.

And my God shall supply all your need according to His riches in glory by Christ Jesus. Now to our God and Father be glory forever and ever. Amen.

Philippians 4:6-7 and 19 NKJV

I believe that God is going to give you wisdom and revelation for the resources or strategy that you need to move forward with your ministry. Do not let your heart be worried; only trust that God has called you to stretch your faith and align with His outlook for your life.

MONEY SAVER TIP

 Work with a non-profit specialist to prepare and file for your non-profit organization. Bylaws, ministry board members and start-up capital is required to be able to complete the application process. Avoid working with people who are unfamiliar or unqualified to help this process go smoothly. It will cost time and money; working with a qualified specialist will be less time and overall less money because they will know the process. Their experience will make the application process less frustrating and time consuming.

A non-profit organization that is recognized by the Internal Revenue Service will be assigned and FEIN or an EIN. (FEIN stands for Federal Employer Identification Number.) When I opened my business account it was done as a DBA. I wasn't sure if I wanted a non-profit ministry or a for-profit business. My work as a consultant, advisor or coach for growing ministries or individuals functions as a for-profit company. I have book sales, speaking and coaching fees, and do not receive donations for what I do.

As a non-profit organization, you must care for every aspect of your ministry and keep a clear distinction between the non-profit and for-profit aspects of what you are doing. There are several ministries that maintain two entities that are financially separate but are managed cohesively. The for-profit entity is the book store product sales, speaker fees and anything that would qualify as a for-profit transaction or exchange. The non-profit entity receives donations and in return, donation receipt letters can be sent out. Both entities can give to non-profit organizations, but it is also good to know that your for-profit business can give donations, resources and support to your non-profit organization. Just as legislation or laws are subject to change, it is necessary to stay up to date with the regulations that concern your non-profit organization. Accurate and properly maintained financial records are fundamentally essential for you. Do not give full responsibility to your spouse or good friend. Inaccurate record keeping will negatively affect the health and longevity of your ministry. Trust and hire a professional and always oversee their work.

ACCURACY IN YOUR MINISTRY ACCOUNTING

Around 2012, an organization overseas was hosting our ministry for a weekend. It was absolutely amazing to visit their country and see how their ministry was growing. The church was an inspiration to me. The layout and function for every space was impeccable. They had seating in their sanctuary for 1500 people. Both Sunday morning services were at capacity. They had classrooms filled with staff and volunteers and a catering team that served lunch after the services for a very low price. They used their childcare classrooms for community outreach. Each room had a different theme and the church would allow parents to rent the classroom to host birthday parties. They had a room for ballet, an indoor gym and a youth room that could seat around 200 people.

This church had grown beyond its current location and was fully established in two other locations. The ministry was reaching the lost and seeing transformation take place in every community they were working in. Until one day they got a final bill notice from their government. Several years prior to our trip to minister with them, their accountant checked the wrong box on a tax form. Subsequently, for several years, the wrong box got marked again and again. By the time the pastors were contacted for the audit and to be informed of their fees and penalties, they owed millions and millions of dollars. The pastors lost their beautiful building that was busting at the seams with growth. They lost their City Centre location and their newly expanded third location. The church that was changing the trajectory of an unsaved country now sits empty with chains on the doors. The pastors have regrouped and have started rebuilding their church. They are meeting for one service on Sunday mornings in a hotel ballroom. They are continuously working to restore their ownership of the church building and City Centre location. Proper accounting could have prevented this situation.

> ## Choose your friends with caution; plan your future with purpose, and frame your life with faith.
> Thomas S. Monson

YOUR MINISTRY INVESTMENT PLAN

When I first started my business, I decided that in addition to giving the 10% tithe, I would save a minimum of 10% of my profits. After that, I could use the remaining 80% for paying work related bills, pay for website development, and pay for continuing education or certification. When it is time to rent a venue for a training event or purchase business coaching, I will have the money available as long as I continue to set it aside.

When starting a ministry, you should establish a financial plan at the start of your ministry. You can decide at the beginning how finances are spent. Before you decide how they are spent, better questions would be:

- Why do I need to establish a financial plan for my ministry?

- Why should I plan to keep my ministry out of debt?

- Why would this plan be more effective from the beginning versus adding this plan after the ministry has grown?

- Why will I be able to do more if I work from a plan?

Let's look at some possible answers to these questions.

WHY DO I NEED TO ESTABLISH A FINANCIAL PLAN FOR MY MINISTRY?

Consider starting with a plan as the beginning of a good habit. We all know that habits can be hard to change once they have been created. Habits help us get things accomplished without having to put a lot of thought or effort into them. Once a habit is created, studies have shown the amount of time it takes to change the habit. One article I read stated that it can take as little as 66 days to change a habit. They also said it could take up to 250 days if you were still working to create that change. For some, they never reach the goal of making a change. Therefore, it is good to start with a plan. You may need to modify it or amend it, but starting with a plan will start the habit of financial planning for your ministry.

WHY SHOULD I PLAN TO KEEP MY MINISTRY OUT OF DEBT?

Debt is easy to get into and can be extremely difficult to get out of. Debt for your ministry would mean that you are spending more than what is coming in, as well as, indicate you are not in the position to give to those in need as their needs arise. Also, just as personal debt can have a negative effect on your peace of mind, the negative effect of financial pressure will increase when you are trying to make ends meet from a deficit.

CAN DEBT BE AVOIDED? IS THAT REALISTIC?

Debt can be avoided! I have seen organizations achieve building plans, purchase land, print resources, host conferences and sustain growth without going into debt. You can build your ministry in such a way that it starts and stays out of debt.

When you start out upside down (in debt), it's an uphill battle to break even. In my ministry training classes, I encourage people to partner with other ministries. Gain support and grow when you're ready. There is no shame in starting small. For example, my very first ministry training class: the week of the seminar I had one registration! Just one! I was on the fence about cancelling it because one registration meant I would be in debt and I would personally have to cover materials I purchased in hopes of more than 20 people registering. At the end of the week, the day before the seminar, I had thirteen people registered. At this, I could pay for the rental and the

> **When you start out upside down, it's an uphill battle to break even.**

materials, as well as cover the cost of having two guests attend without registering. I broke even. There is only one problem with breaking even, there is nothing available to move forward with.

As you build your ministry, use wisdom in planning your events. Learn from the costly mistakes of ministries that are now non-existent because they built too quickly and often ignored their budget. When I first thought of writing this book, I wanted the subtitle to be something like *Protecting Your Ministry from Going Out of Business*. I want the kingdom of God to expand. I want to see nations in revival. I want to see ministry crusades that lead millions of people in a prayer of salvation. Even beyond my heart's desires and prayers, I want to give you the knowledge you need with practical application for fulfillment of the calling on your life and ministry.

Why would financial planning be more effective from the beginning of your ministry versus incorporating this plan five years from now? Let me follow this question with another question; is it easier to stay on course or have a course adjustment? Having a financial plan or spending limit in place will help you prioritize the dollars that you spend. It will create a mindset of kingdom stewardship.

I was talking to a client, who was in the start-up phase of her ministry. She was discussing different issues she was having and trying to find a way to streamline her efforts and achieve greater kingdom impact. When I asked her, what was keeping her from creating this next level of streamlining, she said, "Routine, I guess."

How much of our daily lives is accomplished out of routine or habit? I read an article online that talked about habits, how they are formed and how habits give our brains more brain power for when we need it. I thought that was a fun fact, but the study when on to show how changing a habit can take anywhere from 66 to 250 days. Imagine, you are established in ministry. You finally reached a pivotal goal and you are ready to be home with your family or take a month-long sabbatical. You truly want to rest in His presence, enjoy soaking in worship and hear from God. Even though you have reached a point where you want to take a moment and fully enjoy it without rushing back to emails, phone calls or ministry appointments, you can't do it. Ten years ago, when you started in ministry you opted not to plan for this moment.

> ## If you fail to plan, you are planning to fail!
>
> Benjamin Franklin

WHY WILL I BE ABLE TO DO MORE IF I WORK FROM A FINANCIAL PLAN?

I truly believe that a financial plan in place for your ministry will help you create effective plans for every area of your ministry. You will cautiously look over the cost and worth in your decision-making process. You will understand the value that comes with planning ahead and I believe that just as the parable of the talents demonstrates the blessing on good stewardship, we must be good stewards with kingdom finances.

DESIGNING YOUR HOUSE

PART ONE

A foundation that has been built on a love for God and a passion to fulfill the Great Commission is a great start for your ministry. In addition to the foundation, there are four other key areas for house to stay standing. Just as these areas are key to the establishment of the house, they are vital in order to build and sustain your ministry.

ROOF

The roof over your house provides protection for everything inside. It prevents wind, rain, sleet or snow from getting into your house and ruining your belongings. Just as a roof provides the covering and protection from the external elements, your ministry must have a covering that protects the life and the function of every area in your ministry. God is your covering. He is your shield, support and defender from the enemy. He established His angels around you.

> *God is our refuge and strength, an ever-present help in trouble. Therefore, we will not fear, though the earth give way and the mountains fall into the heart of the sea, though its waters roar and foam and the mountains quake with their surging.*
>
> Psalm 46:1-3 NIV

> *Whoever dwells in the shelter of the Most High will rest in the shadow of the Almighty. I will say of the Lord, "He is my refuge and my fortress, my God, in whom I trust." Surely he will save you from the fowler's snare and from the deadly pestilence. He will cover you with his feathers, and under his wings you will find refuge; his faithfulness will be your shield and rampart.*
>
> *You will not fear the terror of night, nor the arrow that flies by day, nor the pestilence that stalks in the darkness, nor the plague that destroys at midday. A thousand may fall at your side, ten thousand at your right hand, but it will not*

come near you. You will only observe with your eyes and see the punishment of the wicked.

If you say, "The Lord is my refuge," and you make the Most High your dwelling, no harm will overtake you, no disaster will come near your tent. For he will command his angels concerning you to guard you in all your ways;

Psalm 91:1-11 NIV

Just as a roof covers every room in the house, your spiritual covering should be over every area of your ministry. The roof creates a connection from every aspect of the house. It creates a contact point so that every area of the ministry has something outside itself to help govern it. No one builds a house and leaves one room uncovered. Every function or extension of your ministry should be submitted to God's authority and headship for the ministry. Every event, outreach and offering deserves your attention. It should be cared for and watched over as you have been entrusted with each of these aspects of ministry.

In addition to a spiritual covering for your ministry, those that you have qualified to be on your ministry board, will provide a natural covering for your ministry. Your board members should serve as a hedge of protection for all that you are doing in ministry. They should become part of your prayer team and greatest intercessors. They might not be working in the trenches with you, but they should be praying for you and your ministry often. What you are doing as an individual and as a ministry needs to have intercessors who will be disciplined in their prayer life. God has prepared the way for you but that will not prevent the enemy from attempting to distract or derail you from your purpose.

UTILITIES

Could you imagine having company over to your house and letting them find out they couldn't wash their hands or turn on a light? I could not! Water and electricity are two things that I will never want to live without. I will be honest; I don't think I could live in a house without running water or electricity. I need both resources to enjoy where I am and what I am doing. I know that my desperate need for their supply applies to both my natural and my spiritual wellbeing. These resources are just as vital for me as they are for you. The foundation is laid, framing for walls go into place, a roof is installed and then the house comes to life with running water and electricity!

Let the Holy Spirit flow in your ministry like rivers of living water. The Holy Spirit gives nourishment to your spiritual life and your spirit should thirst for it just as your body thirsts for water. The Holy Spirit can supply light through the gift of wisdom and discernment. He can bring clarity to confusion and order to chaos. Consider the consequences from being disconnected from the Holy Spirit. Without it, your ministry will not have what it needs to grow or sustain growth. You could have everything in place, but a ministry that does not welcome the Holy Spirit as part of who God is in the ministry, is a ministry functioning without the power connected or running water.

Just as electricity is a form of energy, the Holy Spirit living inside you is energy. Power up and connect your ministry with the supernatural supply of energy from God. You will discover, the work of the ministry is never finished, but the work of the ministry should always be done to glorify God. If you are exhausted, physically and emotionally drained, constantly fighting off sickness and struggling to make it through each day, take time away from building or expanding your ministry. Take time to restore, recuperate and rebuild your physical and spiritual energy. Walk with God and regain your strength, then when you're ready, return to building and expanding your ministry. If you choose not to, you will see the impact it has on your ability to build or sustain your ministry.

The work or business of ministry should stop when you start to feel the power is fading and the water is slow. You cannot continue to do ministry if your relationship with God or the Holy Spirit is not connected to everything you are doing. If you continue in ministry after the water and electricity has been disconnected, those that you are trying to minister to will begin to suffer. They will feel the effect from a loveless and powerless ministry and as ministers, we must always encourage people in their faith. We must always encourage and strengthen our relationship with God. We must maintain our love for God and do not let our work get in the way.

CAN I AVOID THE DISCONNECT?

Allow the power of who God to connect with every area of your heart, life, relationships and ministry. He loves us and wants to be a part of everything we have going on. He doesn't want to be left out or left behind. Just as water connects to various part of the house and electricity connects to every room of the house, so should your relationship with God connect to every part of who you are and what you are doing.

While you are breathing, you should be actively fulfilling your purpose on earth. The life source to your ministry is dependent on maintaining a powerful connection between you and the Holy

Spirit. God has anointed you for ministry. He has established you for this purpose. His anointing should overflow from your relationship with Him to those you minister to. Just as you enjoy receiving from Him, enjoy sharing it with others. Invite people to connect with the Holy Spirit, just as you would offer your guests water to drink or food to eat.

WALLS

Ministries function at their best when they have taken the time to build a support system that extends to every area of their ministry. Just as walls provide structure and support to a roof, you can create structure and support for your ministry.

A primary support to your ministry is from the participation of your board members. They not only create accountability but also provide strength and support to your responsibility in ministry.

> **A primary support for your ministry is from the participation of your board members.**

Consider this, your board members give support to your ministry by their proximity to what you are doing in ministry. If you talk to them once a year, exchange emails quarterly and send an occasional text message, they may not be providing the support that your ministry needs to stay standing.

I visited a house that had the oddest support beam right in the middle of the kitchen to living room walkway. While I was there, I nearly ran into the beam on several occasions. Mind you, I am not a clumsy person but this support beam was what I considered to be "in the way" of where I was going. Your board members, accountability team, staff or volunteers, provide support for your ministry. Their thoughts and opinions should be taken into consideration when you are building, expanding or updating your ministry. They should not be compared to this one beam or thought of as something "in the way" of your ministry. If at some point, you felt like I did in that house, where the beam kept coming out of nowhere and catching me off guard, you should set a time to meet with that person or group of people. If they are no longer in support of your purpose or if you have changed the vision or mission of the ministry, then instead of looking at them and treating them as if they were in your way, release them from their commitments or obligations to your ministry.

When a board member resigns, then you need to revisit your bylaws and start qualifying a new member. Just as that beam was "in my way," its purpose still existed to support and hold up the roof. You will need to find new support for your ministry. There are several different reasons that could lead to volunteers leaving or board members resigning, the important thing for your ministry to remember is just as God has called you to the ministry, He will call others to support it and support you too.

A secondary support to your ministry will be found in creating ministry partners. Each ministry must take the time to design their own partner program. The program should explain what it means to be a partner, how to become and remain a partner and how that partner provides support to the ministry efforts. It should also be clear on what benefits the partner

A secondary support for your ministry is found in creating ministry partners.

receives from the ministry. In doing so, you are giving back to the partner. When you are starting out, you may be able to hand out a CD or DVD of a message you love or that you have recorded. As your ministry grows, the benefits of partnering with you can also grow.

Partner gifts can be as simple as an email with a free teaching download link. It could be front row seating or early access to events. It can be discounted registration, a copy of your newest book, a t-shirt with your ministry logo on it. You can create levels of partnership and based on their monthly partner gift, then they receive more from your ministry or extended benefits. It is up to you to create your partner program. You can model your partner gift after another ministry and give a similar gift because you love and appreciate it.

Another form of ministry support comes from your volunteers. The people who love you, your ministry and want to be a part of something bigger than themselves. Always love, honor and value your volunteers. Volunteers are partners with your ministry. They give their time to extend and multiply your efforts in ministry. Meet with your volunteers on a regular basis. Build relationships with them so that you are as invested in them as they are in you.

VOLUNTEER TIP: RECRUIT AND ROTATE

 Recruit new volunteers as you continue to develop your active volunteers. When you can, rotate your volunteers to a position of serving that they would like to try out or a new area of learning. When you can, let them attend without serving (if they can even handle that).

This allows them to receive without hesitation or the need to do something else. Plus, always, always, celebrate what your volunteers achieve in your ministry. They are the team members that move the ministry forward and live the ministry in motion.

I love the volunteers at our ministry. They take days off from work, show up early and always stay late. They are faithful, dedicated and trustworthy. Not to mention, they have mastered southern hospitality, which is truly an extension of the heart of our ministry. When you visit us, we want you to feel welcomed to our home. From the cowboy at the front door, through the greeters in the bookstore, to the passion on the worship team, from the message taught by the ministry, we are all here to serve the those in attendance. Our ministry can do so much, on such a big scale, because of the hearts of those who volunteer.

WINDOWS

When I was thinking, and planning this book, God spoke to me the concept that building a ministry is like building a house. I got so excited because of how quickly the outline came together and how there is such a strong correlation for building a house and building a ministry. I quickly laid out every room of the house and how it represents different aspects of ministry.

My mind began to run and my thoughts ran even faster and then I thought about the placement of windows on a house. How do windows apply to ministry? I was stuck for a moment and then the reality of their purpose spoke to me. Ministry should have windows in every room. Windows that are clean and maintained make it possible for you to see what is going on inside. Where a ministry is concerned, windows give you the opportunity to let others see, even from a distance, the good that your ministry is accomplishing.

What would an open window allow for those outside your ministry to see? Just as you could see a family sitting down at dinner, someone watching television, someone playing the piano or reading a book, you can see that an environment conducive to love and growth has been established. It is the same for your ministry. Giving people access to see what is going on in your ministry will increase the ability for your ministry to grow. By giving people the opportunity to see the ministry in motion, they will understand the affect it is having on the lives around it, and most importantly, they will see how the vision is becoming reality.

Create windows into the ministry to help people see:

- what the ministry is doing

- how the ministry is doing what it's doing

- who the ministry is helping

- why the ministry can help

- how the ministry has made the vision, mission or purpose clear

- they can trust, support, and partner with the ministry

CHAPTER FIVE

DESIGNING YOUR HOUSE

PART TWO

PREPARE THE ROOMS OF YOUR MINISTRY

Building a ministry is like building a house. Just as each room of the house has a purpose, so do the rooms or extensions of your ministry. When you plan, and give a purpose to every room in your ministry, you will be able to truly bring your mission statement to life! You get to incorporate who you are, who you want to reach and how you want to do it. We're going to look at the different areas of your ministry and get creative. Be excited about the developing the call of God on your life. Each room in your ministry needs a plan for its development and growth. This plan will not only help you launch a part of your ministry, but it will also provide the ability to sustain it as well. You will be able to articulate functions of your ministry, as well as, the blessing your ministry is to those involved with it.

As you create the plan for each room in your ministry, you will need to create a timeline for making each room available. By defining the role of each room, you will define and establish the focus and the intent of your ministry. In doing so, you will be able to say no to opportunities that will distract or subtract from your calling or your ministry. At this moment, I want you to stop and take a moment, say to yourself: I do not need to decorate every room of the house right now. I will be considerate of God's timing, my timing and I will apply good judgment. I will work with what resources I have and develop what I can. I will believe God to meet my needs and the needs of this ministry. God is more than able to supply my needs. He will send support through encouragers, team members, and partners.

I am an optimistic person. God made me this way. I believe everything is possible and I believe that you will find a way to do what God has called you to. Through building your ministry, applying knowledge, wisdom and discernment, I am confident that God will make a way for you to serve the community around you.

Think back to your first apartment or your first house. When you moved in, did you have all the furniture that you needed? Did you move in having every picture ready to hang? Just as most people move into a house and gradually purchase the decorations or furniture that they need, most likely your ministry will be decorated or developed in stages. You are developing the initial build out and design and with time you'll decorate and expand as you can.

You are building a house of ministry and you are designing the practical function of your ministry. When it's time and you have made each area ready to welcome guests, you will get celebrate and have open house! Every service, every effort in ministry will be like an open house. You will have made a place and made it ready to receive those who are in search of what your ministry can provide for them.

Before every service, our ministry team has a planning meeting. We look at each roll of the ministry and what we need to do to make sure we have everything covered. Even though a lot of the ministry services are similar, we continue to work together to plan. We have also incorporated having a team meeting after the services to discuss what was great and what needs to be worked on. No matter how big, established, or developed your ministry gets, always, always meet with your team and plan. As a team, we celebrate what God is doing in the ministry. As a ministry, we are problem solving to see what we can do even better, together.

A goal without a plan is just a wish.

Antoine de Saint-Exupéry

Next we will work through how you prepare for house guests, meaning those who you invite to experience your ministry.

LIVING ROOM

People love doing life together, whether it's a best friend, family member, or a co-worker. Most people enjoy the company of others. It's true, some people have a hard time being outgoing and some people get nervous in a crowd of strangers or in big social settings. This makes it important to develop an opportunity to fellowship in a small group setting, Sunday school class, or to have a family meal together. Fellowship opportunities are important. You need people to connect with guests at your ministry. People interact with strangers every day. Make your ministry a place where "strangers" can become friends.

Within your fellowship or social opportunities, develop discipleship opportunities and a program. The program could be a series of four to eight weeks, in sixty minute sessions, that use different materials to further develop people's faith providing accountability for growing their personal relationship with God. Take a deep breath. You do not have to be the only one teaching; you do need to know what is being taught and by whom. You can host other teachers, ministers, use ministry DVDs, written resources like workbooks and start a Bible reading plan. You have lots of options and you get to discover which ones will work best for your ministry. Be aware, as it is your ministry, you are fully responsible for those who will sit under your teachings and for the teachings they receive that your ministry hosts.

You have lots of options and you get to discover which ones will work best for your ministry.

Not many of you should become teachers, my fellow believers, because you know that we who teach will be judged more strictly.

James 3:1 NIV

My brethren, let not many of you become teachers, knowing that we shall receive a stricter judgment.

James 3:1 NKJV

Don't be in any rush to become a teacher, my friends. Teaching is highly responsible work. Teachers are held to the strictest standards. And none of us is perfectly qualified. We get it wrong nearly every time we open our mouths. If you could find someone whose speech was perfectly true, you'd have a perfect person, in perfect control of life.

James 3:1 MSG

Dear brothers, don't be too eager to tell others their faults, for we all make many mistakes; and when we teachers of religion, who should know better, do wrong, our punishment will be greater than it would be for others. If anyone can control his tongue, it proves that he has perfect control over himself in every other way.

James 3:1 TLB

I included this one scripture with multiple translations, in hopes that whichever one is your preferred version, the verse might be listed. I am not a perfect person. The only perfect one that existed and walked on this earth is Jesus. I do not use that as an excuse to be imperfect, but I do think of this verse in effort to make better decisions or to guide my moral compass.

KITCHEN

What makes a home? When you think of buying one, what are the top three things that you want the home to have before you buy it? One of them in my top three is the kitchen. Why? The kitchen is where you get to prepare meals for your family and friends. You will give them something that meets their needs for spiritual food and natural food. You get to serve soul food in the best sense of the words.

Preparing and serving spiritual food is like making any meal of the day. Some people will come around needing something simple, like a breakfast bar. It meets their need in the form of a simple energy boost but they won't be around long. Before you know it, they are on their way to where they were headed before they met you.

Preparing and serving spiritual food is like making any meal of the day.

Some people will come around, who will need more support and something more substantial than breakfast. They will be around a little longer. They'll need more encouragement, teaching, discipleship, and get more involved with your ministry. They'll help volunteer, occasionally help clean the kitchen or the living room, but after a little while, you'll realize they are just there for lunch.

Then there is another whole group of people that will come because what you serve for dinner, keeps them coming back for more and more. They love what they ministry is doing. They enjoy the conferences, the outreach, and the volunteering! They enjoy being around the table because they know you're making something that is just for them and everyone they invite to come too! Those that are around your table are the ones who thought they were coming by for a breakfast bar or a sandwich with a bag of chips, but they stayed because you took time to serve them. You took time to see them, understand their position, and meet their needs. Not only do the people around your table enjoy what you're serving, but they take rations with them to meet the needs of those around them.

Just as you prepare something fresh to feed your physical body, you should prepare spiritual food for yourself and those around you. People will not keep coming back to your ministry if you continue to serve leftovers. People are smart and most of them will remember a key point or a message title. Pastors do not have the luxury of telling the same message week after week. The congregants will quickly let them know that it is unacceptable and if the pastor continues to share the same message, the church will cease to exist. If you are building a church and will be pastoring, consider teaching in a series. Most people will not retain more than three points from a message, so if you find yourself with more than three points and less than seven, you have a two-part series. If you have fourteen scripture references and eight points, you can make a three-week series. The Holy Spirit will speak to you through scriptures and you will find that you can teach life application and insight week after week. Ultimately, you are the chef and you will find a way to get cooking in your amazing kitchen.

Evangelists and missionaries have more flexibility in the life span of their messages. Evangelists that have a different audience or physical location are more likely to share the same Holy Spirit inspired message for a season. If you are building this form of ministry, most likely you will be traveling from location to location while ministering to different groups of people. It is important to keep a record of the location and what message you shared. You could have a powerful time of ministry and everyone loved the message, but if you return the following year to give the same powerful message, it may not go over so well. There are two reasons why you would end up giving the same message again:

1. The Holy Spirit impressed upon you in your time of preparation to give the message.

2. Lack of preparation and you're deciding to stick with a message that has previously had a good response.

When you have a ministry invitation, I want to strongly encourage you to prepare for every opportunity. You may have the same scriptures and the same examples, but you can pray and ask God for fresh revelation. You can ask Him for a specific message for those that will be in the service with you. In scripture, we are reminded that "He will never leave us, nor forsake us" and just as that is true in the good times and the bad, He will not forsake us when we are in ministry for Him.

> *I no longer call you servants, because a servant does not know his master's business. Instead, I have called you friends, for everything that I learned from my Father I have made known to you.*
>
> John 15:15 NIV

At that time Jesus said, "I praise you, Father, Lord of heaven and earth, because you have hidden these things from the wise and learned, and revealed them to little children."

Matthew 11:25 NIV

Each office of ministry has a different purpose. Knowing your mission statement, the focus of your ministry, and understanding who you are called to minister to, will help you develop your ministry.

So Christ himself gave the apostles, the prophets, the evangelists, the pastors and teachers, to equip his people for works of service, so that the body of Christ may be built up until we all reach unity in the faith and in the knowledge of the Son of God and become mature, attaining to the whole measure of the fullness of Christ.

Ephesians 4:11 NIV

LAUNDRY ROOM

Any time that you have ministering to people, give them the opportunity to accept Jesus Christ as their Lord and Savior. Walk them through the sinner's prayer and praise God for everyone who becomes a Christian. I love that this is the laundry room of your ministry! Jesus is our ability to become clean and pure; we have forgiveness of our sins and we do not have to spend eternity away from the Father.

Salvation gives people the opportunity to know Jesus. This needs to be a cornerstone for your ministry. I would encourage you, keep salvation encounters at the forefront of your mind for your ministry. You are called to expand the Kingdom of God. Expansion happens through salvation.

> *This righteousness is given through faith in Jesus Christ to all who believe. There is no difference between Jew and Gentile, for all have sinned and fall short of the glory of God, and all are justified freely by his grace through the redemption that came by Christ Jesus.*
>
> Romans 3:22-24 NIV

> *If you declare with your mouth, "Jesus is Lord," and believe in your heart that God raised him from the dead, you will be saved. For it is with your heart that you believe and are justified, and it is with your mouth that you profess your faith and are saved.*
>
> Romans 10:9-10 NIV

> *For I am convinced that neither death nor life, neither angels nor demons, neither the present nor the future, nor any powers, neither height nor depth, nor anything else in all creation, will be able to separate us from the love of God that is in Christ Jesus our Lord.*
>
> Romans 8:38-39 NIV

> *But because Jesus lives forever, he has a permanent priesthood. Therefore, he is able to save completely those who come to God through him, because he always lives to intercede for them. Such a high priest truly meets our need—one who is holy, blameless, pure, set apart from sinners, exalted above the heavens. Unlike the other high*

priests, he does not need to offer sacrifices day after day,
first for his own sins, and then for the sins of the people. He
sacrificed for their sins once for all when he offered himself.

Hebrews 7:24-27 NIV

BATHROOM

In our society, could you call a house a house if it had no bathroom? For most people, the number of bathrooms determines if they will even look at a house, much less buy it. It's the same for your ministry. How often will you give people the time to get spiritually cleaned up? Salvation is the moment that starts the new life of a Christian. It is truly being reborn. For some ministers, they believe that once you are saved, anything that was of the "old self" is gone and it is not a part of who you are as a believer. For other ministers, they believe that the new believer is saved but there is a need to cut off generational curses and have them attend an inner healing session once a week for two months.

You were taught, with regard to your former way of life, to put off your old self, which is being corrupted by its deceitful desires; to be made new in the attitude of your mind; and to put on the new self, created to be like God in true righteousness and holiness.

Therefore, each of you must put off falsehood and speak
truthfully to your neighbor, for we are all members of one
body. "In your anger do not sin": Do not let the sun go
down while you are still angry, and do not give the devil
a foothold. Anyone who has been stealing must steal no
longer, but must work, doing something useful with their
own hands, that they may have something to share with

those in need. Do not let any unwholesome talk come out of your mouths, but only what is helpful for building others up according to their needs, that it may benefit those who listen. And do not grieve the Holy Spirit of God, with whom you were sealed for the day of redemption. Get rid of all bitterness, rage and anger, brawling and slander, along with every form of malice. Be kind and compassionate to one another, forgiving each other, just as in Christ God forgave you.

Ephesians 4:22-32 NIV

I believe that God can do anything. I also believe that for some, salvation can be a "cold turkey" experience. Everything that was a part of their "old self" is no longer an issue or a temptation. They can walk away clean, leaving their old habits and addictions behind. I believe, that for some, as much as they want a "cold turkey" experience, they will need more than that. They might need deliverance, six weeks of inner healing, or a fasting with prayer experience to get free from ties that would pull them away from following God.

It is not up to us as ministers to judge someone and then prescribe a salvation process. We are agents that present salvation. From there, we need a continued process of discipleship. Allow the Holy Spirit to come in and open the eyes of the new believer. The Holy Spirit brings conviction and correction. God does not display His love for us by telling us how bad we were before Him; He does not love with condemnation.

You, however, are not in the realm of the flesh but are in the realm of the Spirit, if indeed the Spirit of God lives in you. And if anyone does not have the Spirit of Christ, they do not belong to Christ. But if Christ is in you, then even though your body is subject to death because of sin, the Spirit gives life because of righteousness. And if the Spirit of him who raised Jesus from the dead is living in you, he who raised Christ from the dead will also give life to your mortal bodies because of his Spirit who lives in you.

Romans 8:9-11 NIV

I wanted to include the entire chapter of Romans 8 because it marks the difference between living in the flesh and living in the spirit with the Spirit of God inside us. I also felt to ask you to take a moment and read it yourself.

Always share the joy of your salvation. As you build your ministry, you will get more and more confident in praying and leading people to Jesus. You will also become more confident on how you can disciple or walk with new believers. Just as they will need you and the help of others to mentor them in their walk with God, you will also need to continue to develop your walk with God and be mentored.

OFFICE

The office of your ministry is where the business of ministry is organized and developed. It is in this room that you make maintaining and sustaining your ministry a priority. There is a high level of accountability to this room in your ministry. It cannot become the "junk drawer" of paperwork or projects that you don't want to work on. How you care for this room will determine the stability of your ministry. How you care for this room will determine if the ministry grows or becomes sustainable.

What does sustainable ministry mean? It means that with the proper care and development it will be able to keep going. It will require less energy or maintenance because you have used regular maintenance and created stability for the overall function of the ministry. Think about the development of sustainable resources and how that would help sustain your ministry. Children are being taught to use sustainable resources all the while, learning about the damage of using resources that are not sustainable. This applies to ministries. Your ministry must create resources that can replenish itself before you use all of them.

I attended a conference with John C. Maxwell and he talked about the most important, first hired position anyone should make. He gave several examples of churches or companies that were not growing because of their lack of organization at the top. He went on to explain that his assistant, and any Executive Assistant, will also be the most important position hired. This is going to be especially true for ministries. If you have the wrong person working in the office of your ministry it will prevent your ministry from growing. To use a corporate word, the wrong person will become the "bottle neck" preventing increase in effectiveness for your ministry.

This position will be like the right hand of the ministry. This position will be like the air traffic control person at the airport – they will determine your course. You can have the biggest vision, the clearest mission statement and all the backing of God and Warren Buffett, but if you have the wrong person attending to the office of your ministry, none of those things will matter. Your ministry will not grow beyond the limits you put on it yourself.

Having the right person, in the right position on your staff, will remove constraints. It will multiply your efforts and it will create momentum. These elements alone will make the business of ministry more enjoyable. This person should also be a buffer between you and distractions. Be careful to balance the responsibility and power of this position. The role of this position is to be your armor bearer and guardian. They should always be respected and honored for the role they play in the growth and sustainability of the ministry. If you have already hired the wrong person for this position, then begin mentoring and training your assistant to become the right person. If mentoring and training does not produce an Executive Assistant, then work together to find the right position for that person. Your Executive Assistant should help you create and maintain order along side you.

In the office of your ministry, you need to keep a copy of your bylaws and your written process and procedures for ministry. You need to have your accounting in order, with proper documentation for expenses or purchases.

MONEY SAVER TIP

This is a time and money saver tip. If an expense cannot give a justifiable answer or it is an undocumented purchase, your accountant will not be happy with you. They will want receipts maintained, turned in, and documented and for all purchases. This will also help you keep track of your expenses and correlate them to an event or ministry expansion. Every receipt should answer these questions:

- **Who** – was there for the transaction?

- **What** – was bought?

- **When** – was the transaction?

- **Where** – did the transaction take place?

- **Why** – is the purchase necessary?

Keep clear records and maintain accountability in every area of your ministry. Display integrity with every decision you make—both personally and in your ministry.

CLOSET

Seeing this on the list, you might already be thinking your prayer room or spiritual warfare room, but no. What is the purpose of the closet? In my house, I have a hall closet that stores winter coats, my beach bag with sunblock, an organizer for wrapping paper, and the vacuum. You might be thinking now that I have a very disorganized closet that has become a "catch all" space with a door that hides the disaster, but I would ask you to think again. What do these things have in common with each other? Your first answer could be nothing, but let me show you their common thread and the purpose of the closet.

Everything in the closet has a specific purpose and function and it is tied to a season or a need. I do not need a coat in the Texas summer, but I will need it in the winter regardless of where I am. I may not need it all the time, but I need to have it at the right time. Some items are in the closet are used more often, but not necessarily every day. Like the vacuum, it is something that I use a couple of times a week. I may not use it every day, but I do need to have access to it.

Your ministry, whether you are a church pastor or traveling evangelist, you need to be ready for the season ahead of you. This does not mean to store your treasures on earth and become greedy. Most people do not realize how the support of the ministry will fluctuate. They will not know that summer financial support typically drops for every single ministry until they are mid-summer and panicking because donations peaked in April and it is July. Your closet is the place to store reserves. Your ministry will be able to sustain itself when it remains prepared for the season that you are not yet in.

This is wisdom. It is applying knowledge of the need for a ministry budget or preparing for the future. Do not be a ministry that fails to plan. Believe God to supply your every need. This is true and necessary, but if you eat the seed in your hand instead of planting it, the harvest that you need will not grow. If you waste or use too freely, the resources that come in during the spring, what will you do for the summer and fall? If you prepare for the season ahead of you, your ministry will not only be able to sustain itself, but it can help sustain families or other ministries in their time of need.

> *Joseph was thirty years old when he entered the service of Pharaoh king of Egypt. And Joseph went out from Pharaoh's presence and traveled throughout Egypt. During the seven years of abundance the land produced plentifully. Joseph collected all the food produced in those seven years of abundance in Egypt and stored it in the cities. In each city, he put the food grown in the fields surrounding it. Joseph stored up huge quantities of grain, like the sand of the sea; it was so much that he stopped keeping records because it was beyond measure.*

> Genesis 41:46-49 NIV

The seven years of abundance in Egypt came to an end, and the seven years of famine began, just as Joseph had said. There was famine in all the other lands, but in the whole land of Egypt there was food. When all Egypt began to feel the famine, the people cried to Pharaoh for food. Then Pharaoh told all the Egyptians, "Go to Joseph and do what he tells you."

> *When the famine had spread over the whole country, Joseph opened all the storehouses and sold grain to the Egyptians, for the famine was severe throughout Egypt. And all the world came to Egypt to buy grain from Joseph, because the famine was severe everywhere.*
>
> Genesis 41:53-57 NIV

Plan for the season ahead of you and give your ministry the opportunity to provide for others in their time of famine or need.

BEDROOM

This room is the life source to the other rooms of your house. Everything that your ministry does will come out of what you do in this room. The bedroom is the part of your ministry that provides space and value on an intimate relationship with God the Father. This is your personal sanctuary and the place that business, finances, and distractions do not get to enter.

This room provides space and places value on an intimate relationship with God.

This place in your life and in your ministry, is where you communicate with God. Sharing with Him your hopes and dreams; sharing the truth of how you feel, how you love Him and need Him. It is a place that is set a part for God to communicate with you. That He can share with you His hope and dreams for your life and ministry. He'll share with you His unending love. He'll speak to your heart and bring peace to your mind. He never removes Himself from us, but just as the widow made room for the prophet (2 Kings 4:10), we must always have a room for God the Father in everything we do.

> *Love the Lord your God with all your heart and with all your soul and with all your strength. These commandments that I give you today are to be on your hearts.*
>
> *Impress them on your children. Talk about them when you sit at home and when you walk along the road, when you lie down and when you get up. Tie them as symbols on your hands and bind them on your foreheads. Write them on the doorframes of your houses and on your gates.*
>
> Deuteronomy 6:5-9 NIV

> *Humble yourselves, therefore, under God's mighty hand, that he may lift you up in due time. Cast all your anxiety on him because he cares for you. Be alert and of sober mind.*
>
> *Your enemy the devil prowls around like a roaring lion looking for someone to devour. Resist him, standing firm in the faith, because you know that the family of believers throughout the world is undergoing the same kind of sufferings.*
>
> *And the God of all grace, who called you to his eternal glory in Christ, after you have suffered a little while, will himself restore you and make you strong, firm and steadfast. To him be the power for ever and ever. Amen.*
>
> I Peter 5:6-11 NIV

As you build and design your house, you make think of other rooms that you want to include. Take time to write down your thoughts for each room. Plan for each room and give each one purpose in your ministry. Invite God in to every room.

Commit to the Lord whatever you do, and he will establish your plans.

Proverbs 16:3 NIV

Faith is the road, but communion with Jesus is the well from which the pilgrim drinks.

Charles Haddon Spurgeon

Become a man or woman of prayer ... Let your heart and mind be kept close to the principal calling of your life, which is to hunger and thirst after God and His righteousness ... let the thoughts and intents of your heart be shaped and guided by time spent in His presence.

-Ravi Zacharias

CHAPTER SIX

CREATING ACCESS TO YOUR HOUSE

DESIGNING AND CREATING CURB APPEAL

Creating access to your ministry is like creating curb appeal for a house. This aspect of your house is what you will use to draw attention to your ministry, how you will attract attendees or members, volunteers and donors. It is important that once you create attention that you manage it properly. Just as planting new flowers or mowing the lawn, this is something you must do over and over again. Your curb appeal will require regular maintenance, care, growth and trimming.

I have found from working with different ministries, that most people want to jump in and look at the designing aspect. They skip ahead of the structure and start with picking colors, designing a logo or purchasing business cards. These things are great and very necessary, but the timing of these things should come after the layout of structure and the mission of your ministry is made clear. The design aspect is where you get to be more creative and make the visual appeal to the public. If you can communicate who you are but have failed to define what you do, gaining support will be stunted.

It's important to pay attention to all the details because in the end the details will make or break you. We talked about the importance of your foundation, your personal position, organization and your inner circle. These are all fundamental elements that will give strength and support to your house of ministry. Once you have laid the groundwork and you are prepared for building you can start letting people know about your ministry and what it hopes to accomplish.

Consider these questions:

- How will people find your ministry?

- How do you share your vision or the mission in motion?

- What will draw people to your ministry?

- How will you let people know what your ministry is doing?

- How will you reach the lost?

- How will you advertise for your ministry?

- How will you create and maintain your ministry brand?

- How will people find your ministry?

Let's look at possible answers to each of the previous questions. Before people will know your ministry exists you need to spend time creating a presence online and different social media channels. Invite people into your process of getting your ordination and post updates on your progress. Let people know you are starting a ministry before it even opens. This can become a tricky spot to navigate. You need to be talking about your ministry but you also need to be in a two-way conversation. Ask people questions to identify how your ministry can benefit them personally. This will also help you identify future partners and volunteers.

One area that causes me to be concerned for the growth or potential of a ministry is found in the name of the ministry. As you are brainstorming and coming up with the name you want to use, type it into Google and into a Word document. If Google comes back with "did you mean…" and it has a suggestion for what you typed, then consider a different name. If you type the name into the Word document and it autocorrects, highlights it or puts a line or squiggle below it, consider a different name. Why would I suggest this? If people hear the name of your ministry and go to Google it and Google recommends a different search, you are making it harder for people to find you.

Just recently I came across three ministries that were having issues with their name, all of which have been in existence for several years. If your ministry has been established for more than a year and people are unclear on the name of it or its purpose, I would consider this a crisis. As one example, one ministry name is written as this-that ministry and sometimes it is this-and-that ministries. This may not seem like a big deal but it demonstrates a lack of clarity which will make the online search for you that much harder.

Avoid using a ministry name that is unclear or has an unusual spelling. Creating one ministry and creating a following (or support) will take time. Creating multiple ministry names or DBAs for a ministry will only not only cause confusion but it can also lead to disengagement. If it looks like you are starting over repeatedly, this could potentially convey the wrong message to your donors. It could come across as if your efforts have failed so you are trying another one. It is good to create consistency and name recognition.

The internet is filled with possibilities! There are millions of web addresses already taken and millions yet to be created. There is the possibility that you find the perfect name for your ministry and every possible .com, .org, .net, .me, .tv, that you would want to use is already taken or even worse, it may be for sale, but for thousands of dollars. I attended a Release the Writer™ conference with Wendy Walters and this is something she has everyone do:

- Start by visiting www.godaddy.com.

- Search first for your personal name by typing your first and last name with no space then click search. Search example: melodybarker

- GoDaddy will let you know if the .com of your name is available. If it is, then you will add it to your cart.

- If your name (or the name of the ministry) is already taken, do not panic. Just get creative. Perhaps add your middle initial or think of other possibilities for the ministry. This is an opportunity to be both creative and strategic.

- There may be more than one extension available as well. If so, they will offer you the opportunity to purchase the .net, .org, .me, and .tv options. If you decide you want one or more of these, you will have the opportunity to purchase them in bulk at the same time.

- Note: it is not necessary to buy all of the options just because they are available. If you are unsure of what your ministry will be doing as far as the way you have filed for your non-profit status, I would recommend purchasing the .com and the .org of your name.

Although you can set up your website using anyone of the previously mentioned endings, initially they were started out with distinct purpose for the public to know the type of company by the end or extension of its website. Here is a handy reference to help you understand the purpose of the various extensions:

- .com: commercial (for-profit)

- .org: non-profit organizations i.e. ministries, foundations, charities

- .net: network-related domains

- .me: personal, individual (great for bloggers)

- .tv: television (media-rich site)

When I searched my name, it was available so I immediately bought it for $2.99. When I went to check out, Go Daddy recommended for me to purchase the domain name for a total of three years. I paid around $20 total. I also have my website domain name set to auto-renew at the end of the three years.

My favorite website to buy domains from is www.godaddy. com. It is easy to search, they have great features and overall, good customer service. You can use several different companies to purchase domains. I highly recommend that you use the same company each time. This will streamline your future needs in website development, domain management, and renewals.

People will need to associate your name with your ministry. I remember one day my grandparents, Charles and Frances Hunter, were going through their mail. My Grandma looked at an envelope and said, "Who in the world is 'White Horse Ministries?'" People will not know or remember who this is. That's why we are Hunter Ministries. People will know from the name who they are getting mail from or who they are supporting."

People need to associate your name with your ministry.

There are several ministries I have worked with that have their non-profit organization as a name like White Horse Ministries and they created a DBA (Doing Business As) First and Last Name Ministries.

For example: City of Light, INC DBA Hunter Ministries

Hearts 4 Him, INC DBA Joan Hunter Ministries

It is not uncommon for a ministry to have or to use a DBA. However, you are building a ministry and you want to keep your name and message clear. Using multiple DBA's can stall momentum and slow your growth for name recognition.

HOW DO YOU SHARE YOUR VISION OR THE MISSION IN MOTION?

People are bombarded by emails, commercials, billboards, pop ups, and app notifications. How do you make your message clear or stand out? Through the internet, you can create unlimited websites, play videos, write blogs, send emails and post status updates. If the world is already inundated with these options how will you craft and distribute your message so it doesn't become part of the existing noise?

One of my favorite causes to share with people is Black and White for Jesus Ministries. Founder, David Wine, from Bartow, Florida has a passion and conviction to see orphaned Haitian children cared for. I follow David's Facebook page closely and am always impressed with everything his ministry is accomplishing. Everyday there are pictures of the children, posts about growth and God's supernatural supply for their needs. There is no doubt in my heart or mind that this ministry is making a difference. When I went to the website, www. blackandwhiteforjesusministries.org, I very quickly understood that this ministry is intentionally working to fulfill its mission statement:

We believe hope starts with Jesus. Our mission is to improve lives through Christian growth, humanitarian aid, and educational resources and assistance. We believe that help starts within the heart by accepting Christ. We believe that no one should be hungry, without clothing or shoes. We believe all should have the opportunity to read and write.

David shares the mission in motion every day. He takes the time to post so that the ministry supporters are up-to-date and nearly up to the minute of what God is doing in the lives of the children. He is in Haiti being a father to the fatherless and showing love to the unloved.

As your ministry grows, be sure to partner with ministries outside of your own. Give to extend the gifts that are received by your ministry. We know that as we give, we plant seeds for the harvest that will be needed in our future.

When you share, what God is doing in your ministry or through your ministry, people will naturally be attracted to it. The humanitarian aid, the food or clean water supply, or even the spirit of generosity for what you are doing will minister to others but you need to find the way that works best for you and create support and a following.

"Imitate me just as I imitate Christ" (Paul in 1 Corinthians 11). Some translations say, "Follow me as I follow Christ." If you are truly following Jesus Christ and pursuing God's plan and purpose for your life, creating followers is a good thing. A bad thing for followers, would mean, that you have mislead or misguided them away from God.

Here are few things you can do right now to start creating a following. It is important to start with options that require time and hold off on spending money until you have to. Develop these steps below:

- Make the message positive – The world has enough bad news available, be the light of the world and share the joy of your salvation (Matthew 5:14, Psalm 51:12)

- Keep the message short - Pretend your supporter or "follower" has 15 seconds of focus for your email, post or video

- Keep the message consistent – Create a signature tag line or phrase as part of your ministry brand so that when people read it that automatically associate with you and what you are doing

- Use Social Media Outlets (keep your "handle" or .com/___ consistent on all platforms)

  - Instagram - a great way to share a positive message with a picture and a headline text

  - Twitter – share a positive message with a very limited amount of words

- Facebook – create events, use Facebook Live for free broadcasting

- Periscope – a Twitter product for live broadcasting

- YouTube – post video messages or use live broadcasting features

- LinkedIn – a Twitter product for connecting businesses, employees and services

  - Create a profile for yourself and list the qualities or attributes of yourself and ministry

  - As you make connections with people, you will receive endorsements for what you do

  - Endorsements are people other than you saying you are qualified to do what you say you can do

- Make it clear from a glance – bullet points, short sentences

- More pictures and fewer words

- Make it compelling

WHAT WILL DRAW PEOPLE TO YOUR MINISTRY?

Before people are interested in your ministry they will be interested in you or your ability to "fix a problem." If they need understanding of the Bible, they will look for someone who breaks down scriptures in a way they can understand it. If they want to learn to prophesy, they will search for someone who is accurate and flows in the prophetic gift. Their needs will inspire their searching. If you have made it clear that your ministry can be the answer or offer to help their search for a solution, they will find a way to connect with you.

Undoubtedly, people will be drawn to the Jesus inside you and the Holy Spirit at work in your life. Once they are drawn to you by the Holy Spirit, personal relationships with them and caring for them as people will help keep them connected with your ministry. The "who" you are and the "how" you treat people will either draw people to want to connect with you or it will push them away from connecting with you. This is one of the reasons why churches have placed so much emphasis on community, life groups, home teams, small groups, etc. The relationship factor is key in building a ministry that withstands the test of time. Ultimately, people must like you and connect with you to care about what your ministry is doing.

HOW WILL YOU LET PEOPLE KNOW WHAT YOUR MINISTRY IS DOING?

This will be a question that as time moves forward, the answer will progress and continue to change. What works best today will not always be what works best. A decade ago, mailing long support letters to every donor was the only way to gain additional support and let people know what your ministry had been doing. Now, you have access to multiple social outlets, live streaming, email, and text messaging. All of these resources are in addition to mailing a letter and sending it through the postal service.

This is where you must roll up your sleeves and do some fine tuning. In the beginning, you will need to try, test and prove multiple ways to communicate what your ministry is doing. Start with understanding and getting to know your demographic as it develops. As people start to like your Facebook page or follow you on Instagram or Twitter, you can look at the insights available. The insights will give you information on your demographic.

When you know more about who you are reaching, you will also get to know that how you're reaching them is working. For example, if the larger portion of your demographic has found you on YouTube, then continue to invest time making and posting videos but if you have more people responding to what you post on Twitter, then continue to develop your posts for Twitter. Continue to build each platform, as each platform will reach a different audience.

Some of my favorite posts to see on social media come from Matt and Stephanie Sorger. They post faith-increasing, prophetic and encouraging words in addition to ministry events (see their posts on www.twitter.com/mattsorger). Uplifting, encouraging communication filled with testimonies, updates, ministry growth and ways to connect with you will be what you want to focus on. It is important to invest yourself into communicating with those who have connected or engaged with your ministry.

HOW WILL YOU REACH THE LOST?

As a ministry, you cannot assume that everyone in your service, attending your church or even visiting is already a Christian. Focusing on outreach as well as discipleship should be a core value of your ministry. If every ministry continued to focus on new converts in addition to their continued ministry efforts, the Kingdom of God would explode on the earth!

When I first started in ministry, I focused on salvations. I wanted to see people saved, hearts healed and lives changed. Somewhere in the middle, I got distracted. I still focused on miracles, but attendance, exposure, growth and moving forward started to take my focus. For a year or so, I didn't lead anyone to the Lord. I was attending a conference that was hosted by Patricia King and as I listened to the speaker share her heart for youth finding Jesus as their Lord and Savior, I repented! It stirred in me a desire to see the lost saved. From that moment on, I have been very quick to listen to the Holy Spirit guide me through a "call for salvations." Even when it makes me nervous, I know to trust Him and say what He has me say. Previously, I had made the mistake of assuming everyone that was coming to our Christian conference center would already be a Christian. From that day, I have listened and prayed the sinner's prayer when the Holy Spirit stirs my spirit and every time there is always at least one person to get saved or rededicate their lives to the Lord.

I want to share an awesome salvation story with you. We had a ministry service and it was a night that the Holy Spirit told me to have a call for salvation at the end of praise and worship. As I got up to speak, the Holy Spirit gave me the words to say and the words to pray. I didn't see any hands go up but I never know if it is for someone in the room or someone watching online. After the service was over and the prayer team was wrapping up all the prayer requests, a young girl, around 17 years old came over to talk to me. She had been on the computer earlier that day and used Google to search using the words "healing pain." Our website came up and she clicked on events. She could see that we were having a healing and miracle service that night and convinced her grandmother to drive her nearly an hour from where they lived to come to the service. That night she was healed but before she got healed she got saved! This happened within a few weeks of me refocusing and listening to the Holy Spirit when he says "call for salvation."

HOW WILL YOU ADVERTISE FOR THE MINISTRY?

As a new ministry or if you are updating the way you do ministry, start with researching what is working the best for ministries that are like yours. If you are starting a church, the children and youth program is going to be your target for the highest investment of your time and budget. I have known so many parents who openly admit they don't love their church but continue to attend that church because their children love it.

Let's look at the hands-down, most cost-effective and successful form of advertising for your ministry. Word of mouth is the best form of advertising! It is the best way to create a buzz about your ministry and what it's doing. In the number of times that we have purchased a page in a magazine, rented billboards, paid and sent an email with a larger ministry, we have always seen that word of mouth or a personal invitation has been the most influential form of event invitation that leads to measureable response or results.

Word of mouth from friends, family and co-workers is the most trusted source for businesses to increase brand awareness, increase engagement and even increase sales. You can learn more about word of mouth from books and online resources but here is something interesting I found while researching this topic: **84% of consumers** say they either completely or somewhat trust recommendations from family, colleagues, and friends about products and services —making these recommendations the highest ranked source for trustworthiness.[1]

Word of mouth will always start because of a good or bad experience. As people encounter you, whether it is at the store, the gas station, your ministry service or at a restaurant, their interaction with you can turn into a topic of conversation they have later that day.

I remember going to dinner with friends who were very particular in how they liked to have their meal served to them. They would point out their cup was half-empty or empty and for how long they waited for it to be refilled. They would comment on the amount of time they sat at the table waiting for their server to come to them and take their order for dinner. It would go on and on. Each and every thing that could be commented on would receive a narrative. It was exhausting. What made it even worse is their occupation as pastor or minister would become a topic at the table. To me, this would be the last place to mention what they did for a living.

On one specific occasion, that I truly just wanted to enjoy dinner with a pastor and his family, I gave the hostess $10 to give to our server before they even got to our table. I told the hostess to tell our server, "Keep his glass full and there will be plenty more where this came from." As our server came to the table with a big smile on her face I couldn't help but smile too. The dinner was perfect. The glass stayed full, the server was gracious and friendly, and most importantly the people I was at dinner with commented on how great the dinner went. Granted, this is just dinner but people will notice the difference between who you are on and off the platform of ministry.

Inconsistency will create a negative impact on your ministry. Who you are in your public ministry should be the same as who you are in your home or private life. If there is a difference between who you are when you are watched and not watched, it will find its way to the public and eventually become a word of mouth nightmare. Make every effort to be consistently nice, considerate and Christ-like in all situations. No one is perfect but it is important to always follow to the golden rule: treat others as you would like to be treated.

> **At the end of the day people won't remember what you said or did, they will remember how you made them feel.**
>
> Maya Angelou

HOW WILL YOU CREATE AND MAINTAIN YOUR MINISTRY BRAND?

Let's start by defining the word brand and see how it applies to your ministry.

DEFINITION

BRAND: *Unique design, sign, symbol, words, or a combination of these, employed in creating an image that identifies a product and differentiates it from its competitors. Over time, this image*

becomes associated with a level of credibility, quality, and satisfaction in the consumer's mind. Thus, brands help harried consumers in crowded and complex marketplace, by standing for certain benefits and value. Legal name for a brand is trademark and, when it identifies or represents a firm, it is called a brand name.[2]

Inside your brand we will look at creating the following:

- Logo

- Protecting your brand standard

- Business cards and stationary

- Direct mail marketing

- Email marketing/follow up

- Marketing strategy

- Social Media

- Advertising

DEFINITION

 **LOGO**: *Recognizable and distinctive graphic design, stylized name, unique symbol, or other device for identifying an organization. It is affixed, included, or printed on all advertising, buildings, communications, literature, products, stationery, and vehicles. Not to be confused with a brand, which identifies a product or family of products.[3]*

In your ministry, you will determine what your logo looks like. Elements of the logo will include a picture or words. I would Google popular or easily recognized logos to get a better visual. When I was researching, one of the most impressive was an article on the *50 Most Iconic Brands of All Time*. It was interesting to see how many logos included the name of the company. There are also several companies that show the initial brand logo and the progression or changes made as the company became more well known.

You will also decide how your logo is placed or displayed on all your resources, print outs, flyers, etc. Protecting your brand standard concerning a logo would place a high value on keeping your logo consistent in its style and use.

There was a ministry I was working with and they printed out fifty flyers for an upcoming event. When I saw the flyer, I will be honest and tell you, the look of it made me upset. The layout in general was good. The design as far as color or image chosen for the advertisement could have been more visually appealing. The part that made me upset was the logo itself was pixelated. What does that mean? That means that the logo and the most visually recognized piece for the ministry itself was a low-quality image that was fuzzy and was not the original logo file used for this printing. I immediately said to throw them away and update the flyer with a brand standard logo.

You might say that was a bit dramatic or uncalled for but this is an area of excellence that most ministries sacrifice. They will look at the cost of fifty pieces of paper and consider that to be more valuable than protecting their brand standard. In my opinion, the lack of priority that ministries give to a brand standard will be one of their biggest causes of setback or hindrance to growth. Keep the printed pieces, online pieces and social media images for your ministry look consistent with your ministry.

Recently I was consulting a client who was launching into full-time ministry. We scheduled several one-on-ones to go over what the needs of the ministry were and what part she needed to develop versus what part she need to hire a professional to develop. I found out on our first call, she had already outlined and identified the following:

- her ministry vision and mission

- the primary audience she wanted to reach

- how she was going to reach them

From there, we could focus on who she needed to connect with for logo creation and updating her website. One of the areas that she struggled with was creating quality advertisements that were consistent with what she wanted her brand to say. Discovering this was her weaker area, I recommended that she reach out to a graphic designer and have someone with the right skill set be the answer to her dilemma.

I am all for doing as much of this as you can. When it comes to an area that you are unfamiliar with or an area that you have identified as a weakness, it does not mean that you cannot accomplish what you are working on. It means that because you have identified it as a weakness, that you will hire, barter, or invest the time needed to develop your skills.

God created us to need each other and to work with each other. It is not meant for one person to be able to do it all. Most ministries are and will continue to be led by the visionary personality. The visionary will give ideas and speak to the direction that the ministry should go in, while its weakness will continue to be in giving the details or strategy on how to accomplish the vision. God did not add "Do it all by yourself" when He called you to the ministry.

> **If you're doing it alone, you're doing it wrong.**
>
> John C. Maxwell

MONEY SAVER TIP

For more information and support in identifying and creating your brand, read *Marketing Your Mind* and work through the *Brand Profile* available from wendykwalters.com.

DEFINITION

BUSINESS CARDS: *A standard 2x3 inch card that displays contact information for an individual employed by a company. Business cards typically include a person's name, e-mail address, phone number, website, and company name. They are often used at networking and corporate events to provide other individuals with an easy source for retrieving contact information.[4]*

Your business card should include your logo in addition to your contact information. One way to keep your costs lower is work with a graphic designer and purchase a design package with several pieces at the same time. Once you have found someone to create your logo, have them develop your business card at the same time.

MONEY SAVER TIP

When you need a piece created, before you hire a graphic designer, see if they have packages (of pieces) or bundles (of time) available. If you only need one image made, then you will pay the full cost for that image. What I have done to save money is explain what I need it to say, what I want it to look like and then I put that piece in the package or arrangement to buy future pieces. This will reduce the cost of the one image.

MONEY SAVER TIP

If you do not know your budget, or the amount of money you are willing to spend on a piece, the graphic designer will tell you what they charge for it. When I pay for images that I need for social media or my website, I start with saying, "I need a product image for… and I can pay $-$$$ for the piece." I will list the amount of money I am willing to spend at the beginning of the conversation and by doing so, I am letting the designer know this is how much I have and they can decide if they can do the work on my budget.

DEFINITION

DIRECT MAIL MARKETING: *A method in which carefully targeted prospects (chosen with specific criteria) are presented with custom tailored offers for goods or services via ordinary mail or email. Marketing firms usually 'rent' lists of prospects*

from mailing list compiling firms who maintain a large inventory of names and addresses of prospects, divided into hundreds of categories and sub-categories.[5]

Direct mail is mentioned so that you will know that it is available when you are ready to pay for advertising. Purchasing advertising on this scale can be done when you have completed all your set up and have something specific to advertise like:

- Now Open with service times and community benefits

- Targeting new people to your area

- Outreach event like an egg hunt at a community park or on your ministry property

- Larger special events like guest speakers or hosting another ministry

Email marketing can be a low to no cost way to communicate with your supporters. There are several options available that do not have a monthly or annual fee. The no to low cost will be dependent on how many email subscribers you have. The fewer the number, the lower the cost.

Each email that you send out should be consistent in the way it looks and sounds. When you identify your brand, and design your logo, you will also narrow it down to what colors you use most often. Branding does not mean if your logo does not have blue you can never use blue, but your logo and brand should help you use the common colors found in your logo.

Inside your email, you should always include ways for people to connect with you. Your phone number, mailing address, and social media channels. Make it as easy as possible, just short of giving your cell phone number out, for people to connect and communicate with you. You can maintain a healthy boundary while still being personal and reachable.

MONEY SAVER TIP

When you are first starting out, include your name, ministry name, email and website on things you hand out. Why? Physical address and phone numbers are subject to change faster than you can give out your 500 business cards, 1000 note pads or 5000 pieces of stationary. Also, you want to make sure you give people information that will not change based on your own physical address.

My grandparents wrote more than seventy books while they were alive. Initially they published them with their first ministry's physical address. Then their address changed, it changed again, then they moved again and again, then they got a PO Box. Looking at some of the books that we still have, I can find three different addresses that are not their existing mailing address. Books that were released closer to their passing got the PO Box address printed on them. Some of their books have stickers over the old addresses and some reprints were never updated. They have CD and DVD covers that need to be updated because they haven't had their Porter, Texas address in more than 10 years.

DEFINITION

MARKETING STRATEGY: *An organization's strategy that combines all of its marketing goals into one comprehensive plan. A good marketing strategy should be drawn from market research and focus on the right product mix in order to* achieve the maximum profit potential and sustain the business. The marketing strategy is the foundation of a marketing plan.

Before purchasing any form of advertising, start with research. Research and find out what is most likely going to give you the measurable results you are looking for. Plus, define the measurable results before buying advertising.

Before purchasing any form of advertising, start with research.

Years ago, we purchased a one page ad in a Christian magazine that has a massive subscription. I considered the reach of the magazine and advertised an event that we host twice a year. This way, if people couldn't make it to one of them, they at least had a second option. Plus, I considered the attendance to one or both and hoped that a measureable response would show up in the number of people attending the conference. At every event, we ask people how they found out about the service or the conference. Word of mouth always beats any other form of advertising, including direct mail, direct email and social media posts.

The first event date advertised came and went. We did not see an increase in phone calls, attendance or ordination graduates from the one page ad we place. Amazingly enough, the salesman convinced me that is was the type of event advertised or the overall style of the ad that made the ad not perform well. With this information, I purchased a second ad and listened to what the magazine said would produce more of an ideal measureable response.

The magazine has a large audience that was in line with our target audience. The goal of the ad was to increase our mailing list by offering a free book. Their distribution is worldwide and I was convinced that because they said that ads like ours would be beneficial for the ministry that we would see the results we wanted. We submitted the ad, the magazines went out and within a month we received a total of 200 orders for the book. You might be excited for 200 new names and addresses to be in the data base and excitement is the right attitude until you find out that the magazine went to more than 110,000 homes, churches and businesses. Two hundred means that less than one percent responded to the ad.

To this, I told the ad agent our ad failed. Their response was that we "can't judge the magazine to pass or fail on one ad." I defined it as a failure because I knew the measureable response I was looking for was not achieved. I based the measureable results on how much the placement and cost of the ad and I expected 1,000 people to respond to it. I was hoping for 1%.

Every dollar that comes in to your ministry must be as effective as possible. Avoid purchasing advertisements until it is the only remaining option for growth. At that, I want to reiterate to know your ideal audience, where they are located and research what will be the best way to reach them.

ENDNOTES

1. https://www.getambassador.com/blog/word-of-mouth-marketing-statistics.

2. Definition of brand found at: http://www.businessdictionary.com.

3. Definition of logo found at: http://www.businessdictionary.com.

4. Definition of business cards found at: http://www.businessdictionary.com.

5. Definition of direct mail makreting found at: http://www.businessdictionary.com.

6. Definition of marketing strategy found at: http://www.businessdictionary.com.

CHAPTER SEVEN

CREATING YOUR BACKYARD

You are building a ministry and we have covered the purpose for each room in your house. Now, let's step outside and make some plans for the backyard. I want you to think of the backyard as the outreach efforts or community impact of your ministry.

> He said to them, "Go into all the world and preach the Gospel to all creation. Whoever believes and is baptized will be saved, but whoever does not believe will be condemned. And these signs will accompany those who believe: In my name, they will drive out demons; they will

speak in new tongues; they will pick up snakes with their hands; and when they drink deadly poison, it will not hurt them at all; they will place their hands on sick people, and they will get well."

After the Lord Jesus, had spoken to them, he was taken up into heaven and he sat at the right hand of God. Then the disciples went out and preached everywhere, and the Lord worked with them and confirmed his word by the signs that accompanied it.

Mark 16:15-20 NIV

WHAT OUTREACHES CAN YOU THINK OF THAT MEET THE NEEDS OF A LOCAL COMMUNITY?

How have they established and sustained change or Kingdom expansion? The first one I think of is "The Bridge Ministry" in Nashville, TN (www.bridgeministry.org). They are not the only ministry that serves the homeless community, but they have been doing it since 2004 and have grown beyond serving the homeless. They have a weekly ministry service, a warm meal prepared for an average attendance of 300-350 people, and they have become a food bank that provides for other local ministries. The mission statement for The Bridge Ministry is:

> **To educate those without high school diplomas and job skills to integrate them back into the work force, to bring awareness to hunger and homelessness, and to motivate people to be passionate for the poor.**

HOW CAN YOUR MINISTRY START AN OUTREACH PROGRAM THAT MAKES A DIFFERENCE?

- Identify the needs of your community

- Create a plan to meet the need

- Form a team

  - Establish the "boots on the ground"

  - Raise awareness of the need

  - Raise financial support to supply for the needs of the outreach

  - Recruit resources and donations of items like: clothing, shoes, diapers, sleeping bags

  - School supplies

  - Medical supplies: bandages, ointments, and creams

- Promote the plan

- Position your team

- Start and stay consistent with all efforts in the outreach

- Trial and error will help you find the best way to do outreach

HOW CAN YOUR MINISTRY BE A SAFE-HAVEN OR ALTERNATIVE OPTION FOR RECREATION?

A great answer to this comes with the example from a youth outreach program in Brooklyn, NY. The youth pastor at an inner-city church hosts basketball tournaments on Friday and Saturday nights. The gym is open all night and teams are made from the more than 200 youth that show up weekly. They play all night and the gym is a safe place for the young adults to hang out. Before the games begin, the youth pastor opens the night with the house rules and a short devotional. The young adults know they must watch their language and respect each other. They play game after game until there is one team that is undefeated. It makes for late nights and long days, but for this youth pastor, he knows he is "keeping kids off the streets, out of clubs and out of jail."

WHAT ACTIVITIES CAN YOU BE A PART OF TO DRAW PEOPLE TO YOUR MINISTRY?

Get involved with the city you are in. Go to grand openings, meet and greets, and attend local events. Consider having a booth at the fair or festival. You would be surprised at the number of people who will wander into your booth to sit down and enjoy being out of the sun. Find something like a painter, cartoon artist or balloon animal artist to attract attention. Children will help lead the way – because who can turn down a free balloon animal?

It doesn't have to be expensive or over the top; get creative and think about what would make you want to take a break at a booth. You can have free giveaways and drawings for prizes. The options are endless, but it will be up to you and your team to dedicate the time necessary to prepare an incentive and attract attention to your booth. Plus, with the drawings and giveaways, you can get names or emails and contact the people after the event is over. You can let them know (by inserting an informational handout with the prize) who you are, what your ministry does and where you are located. Let them know that you are there to help them and serve their community.

People who need help will reach out to you after they have exhausted all other options. It may be months before you hear from some and for others, they will check out the ministry and what it is doing before they connect with you. Keep in mind, you are in outreach mode. They need to know that you care for them more than you care about increasing attendance or hitting a goal.

> ## Nobody cares how much you know, until they know how much you care.
>
> Theodore Roosevelt

As you expand different parts or functions of your ministry, never sacrifice the excellence of one area to expand another. This applies to every effort you make in ministry. Do not continue to do something if your heart is not in it 100%. If you work with the homeless because you feel like you must, then stop. You can value a form of ministry and support it, without pretending that you want to do it.

Never sacrifice the excellence of one area to expand another.

I served several Tuesday nights at The Bridge Ministry. I enjoyed going and helping with the team of volunteers that loved serving meals, setting up chairs and caring for the homeless people. I went because I felt like I needed to go, but I came to realize my heart was not in the hands-on. I found that I really enjoyed raising support and awareness for the ministry and that was something I was good at doing. One year for my birthday, I asked that everyone coming to the party to bring a sleeping bag instead of a gift for me. That day twenty-two sleeping bags came to the party and the following Tuesday night, The Bridge Ministry could give sleeping bags to their homeless friends.

Outreach is not always about being the one to go and do. You can support the outreach efforts of other ministries, which will strengthen and multiply their efforts while increasing their impact. Find an outreach that pulls at your heart strings and then find a way to support it with your time, talent or resources.

Life's most persistent and urgent question is, "What are you doing for others?"

Martin Luther King, Jr.

While writing this book, I thought about all the ministries that I have had the pleasure of working with. It is amazing to see how the same message of Jesus Christ can be shared all around the world in different ways. Saying "yes" to the call of God on your life and saying "yes" to being in the ministry requires action more than words.

For some of you, ministry will mean starting a new job as a minister. While for others, it means you will be supporting and volunteering for those in full-time ministry. Then for others, you could be in the middle of these two options. You will be in between a full-time marketplace or secular employment and full-time ministry. Knowing the time or season to move from one to the other, if that is what you desire, will need strategic planning for that transition. It is not a light switch that flips quickly from one position to the next. Plan and build your ministry with God leading the timeline. Maintain your focus on fulfilling the plan and purpose He has given you for your life and ministry.

The ability to build and sustain your ministry is strongly connected to the community that you have around you. Relationships with other leaders in ministry will inspire you to keep going. Surround yourself with Christians who will encourage you and that you can encourage to be intentional with your personal relationship with God and those you serve ministry. There will always be people that you connect with because you are not only drawn to the Holy Spirit inside of them, but your hearts connect as true friends.

This is what it is like for my friends, Dan and Linda Wilson, co-founders of SMM or Supernatural Marriages and Missions. (www. supernaturalmarriage.org). I love Dan and Linda! I love their passion for nurturing healthy, Christian marriages and I love their heart for serving and ministering to the widow, orphan, rejected and abandoned. God has established their ministry to share His love around the world.

Together, their ministry was "created to encourage Spirit-led intimacy in marriages through speaking, teaching, writing and personal counseling. They love going around the USA and to the nations as marriage missionaries. Dr. Dan was an eye surgeon for many years helping thousands with their physical vision. Now Dan and Linda cast the vision of supernatural marriage to the worldwide bride of Christ. They have been married thirty-three years and reside in Fort Worth, Texas." Before completing this book, I wanted to ask Dan and Linda for insight into their journey of ministry and missions.

HOW DID YOU DISCOVER MISSIONS? OR CHOOSE TO FOCUS ON MISSIONS?

Dan and Linda started in missions in 1988 through medical missions. They were used to working and serving in 3rd world countries and through this they were able to share the love of Jesus with those receiving aid. For a period of time, they shifted their focus to marriages. They started teaching in conferences or services about marriage and people started getting saved. God was drawing people in and they were finding salvation, even though they weren't teaching a message of salvation. The Holy Spirit guided Dan and Linda to take Supernatural Marriage out of its box and expand it to include missions. Dan said during our conversation, "Our purpose in the kingdom is bigger than just one focus." Now they have a ministry that works together with churches or organizations around the world. Every time they minister, they see healing and restoration for marriages; they see salvation, deliverance and miracles everywhere they go.

> **Your purpose in the kingdom may be bigger than just one focus.**

HOW WOULD YOU ENCOURAGE NEW MISSIONARIES TO RAISE SUPPORT FOR THEIR TRIPS/MINISTRY?

Their answer was, "Pray a lot!" They encouraged me to "know your passion." They have a true passion for going and doing. Dan went on to say, "God will use your passion to get people excited to help to support you through donating and praying."

Be faithful to God and see His faithfulness provide. Be faithful with what God has given you and be trustworthy with what people give you.

Dan and Linda Wilson

DO YOU DESCRIBE YOURSELF AS BEING IN FULL-TIME MINISTRY?

Their answer was beautiful and could be a key for building or sustaining your ministry. Dan spoke of Apostle Paul, who was a tentmaker before he was a disciple. Dan said, "About 20% of our time is spent as 'tentmakers.' We are entrepreneurs, we run a business, and I work as a physician … 'Tent making' has made a way to a do a lot more in missions that what I thought we could do. We get to spend about 80% of our time in missions."

Ministry may be the place of your express passion, but in order to function in that ministry it may require you to continue working to supply the funds to do the work of ministry. This could be working for someone else or starting an entrepreneurial venture and allowing the profits from your business to provide income to support your vision. Everything you do is ministry if you are doing it with a heart for God and your passion is clear.

WHAT MADE YOU CHOOSE MISSIONS OVER EVANGELISM?

Their answer to this question was, "Missions and evangelism are partnered together." Linda then told me a great story of a man wanting them to come to their house to pray with his family. He was so confident that his family would become Christians, that he had a photographer there to capture the moment they all said "yes"! Linda went on to say beautifully, "Evangelism came to us. What started out as meeting needs from a mission position, became an opportunity to evangelize."

HOW WOULD YOU ADVISE SOMEONE WHO IS STEPPING INTO MINISTRY AND PURSUING MISSIONS?

Their answers were so clear and succinct, I wanted to share them with you as a list:

- Pray a lot!

- Have a strong intercessory team you can lean on for prayer and see fruit produced.

- Be flexible.

- Pray for God to send you.

- Be compassionate—have a heart of compassion for the poor and needy.

HOW DO YOU CONNECT WITH HOSTING CHURCHES?

For Dan and Linda, most of the ministry services they do come from people contacting them and inviting them to minister. This question applies to most ministries. Connecting meaningfully with others is vital to the success of your ministry.

Let people know what you are doing. Share what God is doing in your life and through your ministry, but wait for the invitation to come to you. Being invited to do missions versus pursuing invitations will lead to smoother ministry services. It is much easier to be someone's guest than to invite yourself to be their guest. Arrangements and communication tends to be clearer when there are fewer negotiations to be made.

Always, always, pursue God. Ask Him to bless and expand your ministry. It is our efforts in alignment with His will that make ministry and missions possible.

As fishers of men, we were created to be woven together as a net.

Networking is vital to ministry success, but unlike in business where you simply join professional associations, in the kindgom you rely on the Holy Spirit to lead you in forming connections and developing relationships. This becomes your net ... and it works!

Wendy K. Walters

CHAPTER EIGHT

PLANNING YOUR OPEN HOUSE

E vent planning is where most people want to start building their ministry. It's exciting to be ministering and accepting speaking invitations. It is even more exciting to get to a place where you can host other ministries. Building your ministry with events versus building your foundation is like having an open house or party before unpacking or even moving in.

Skipping the planning stage or rushing through the process of building a strong foundation, you run the risk of putting the cart before the horse, or in this case, the house party before the purchase. You could be building a ministry that does not have what it needs to become sustainable.

DO NOT DESPISE THE DAY OF SMALL BEGINNINGS

When you are ready to start hosting events, start small. There is no shame in starting small. I always encourage people stepping into ministry to start from a position of covering everything yourself. Meaning, if you had to personally cover every expense of a meeting, how much would you spend? At what amount, would you stop spending?

There are a couple of organizations I have helped with who do not start with a max spending budget in mind. They do not consider the final cost before giving themselves a spending limit. This is a dangerous place to be. In ministry, although you are a non-profit organization, this does not mean you can't be profitable.

Hear me clearly on this. Your ministry is a non-profit organization, which means that you or your board members cannot personally make a profit. Your organization can be profitable. Meaning, you are spending less than your outgo.

If you host a ministry service and spend $2,000, then receive an offering of $400, you are $1600 upside down. If you spend $2,000 on hosting your ministry service, receive $1000 in the offering, and have $400 in registration, you are still at a deficit. This is business of ministry that gets the most organizations in trouble.

For example, we were hosted by an out of state organization. The host agreed to pay for two plane tickets, two hotel rooms and let us receive an offering. The venue was a hotel because we were hosted by a ministry that did not have its own building or partnership with a church. The services were held in a large ballroom that could seat 300 people. The host charged $35 per person for registration and it included a light lunch on the day of the event. We set up the bookstore and got ready for the two services. When it was time for the doors to open, a few people came in. A little bit later, a few more people arrived. At the start of service, there were thirty people in the room – including the hotel staff for the event. Are you wondering what was happening? I looked around the room and thought to myself: *How many people registered? I hope more people show up. I hope this ministry has the money to cover this ...*

The thought of the total bill that the ministry agreed to pay nearly stressed me out. Our host had been in ministry for around fifteen years and I knew that she knew how to plan a ministry event. I assured myself that she knew what she was doing and that she had it all worked out. During the afternoon break, she explained to me the position she was in and that is when I got concerned. She put this event on her personal credit cards. She borrowed money to make the event happen. She went on to explain how much debt she was already in. Then shared that when the event was getting closer and the registration numbers were not that high, that she knew she would be in a great deal of trouble if God didn't do something.

The ministry part of the services, where people were healed and delivered was amazing. The testimonies that came in for weeks and weeks after the service were extraordinary. One year after the event a man called to give us a piece of his mind because he knew the organizer of the ministry service and he wanted to condemn us for agreeing to go and minister with her. He went on and on about how she went into debt over the two services. He wanted to make it clear that it was our fault that she was in the position she was in. He wanted us to be ashamed of ourselves.

After giving him time to say what he wanted to say I explained that her personal finances and ministry finances were not something that he should be discussing with us. We were her ministry guests. The arrangements for hosting us was something that she agreed with six months before the event date. We did not request a large or luxurious hotel or ballroom for the ministry services. We simply said "yes" to the invitation for two services on one day with her. What the gentleman did not know (and we were not at liberty to say), was a couple of months after the ministry services with her, a large donation was given to her. The donor specifically gave her money to pay off any personal debt and gave the ministry a donation to get it out of debt as well.

I can feel the sigh of relief that you just experienced. I had the same sigh of relief while I was living through the experience the first time. For a while I took on the responsibility and the weight of the worry for what she was going to do. How was her ministry going to survive? How was she going to make it? I did come to my senses and the truth that we did not put her in that position. She did it to herself. Whether it was in the planning or the lack of budgeting, she understood what she was planning through the whole event. She made the mistake of planning her budget on last minute registrations or people showing up the day of the event. Neither of which happened.

I have two reactions to the story, the first is YEA GOD! God supernaturally supplied an amazing miracle of debt reduction. God gave this ministry the opportunity to operate debt free! My second reaction is more of a warning for you and for others in ministry. It is irresponsible to spend or create debt with the safety net hung on the promise that God will always supply for your needs.

ALWAYS BE FAITHFUL

People in ministry should make their efforts like that of the first people in the parable of the talents. We each are entrusted with a certain amount of talent. We must be faithful with what we have been given and with good stewardship we will see it multiply into more.

> *"Again, it will be like a man going on a journey, who called his servants and entrusted his wealth to them. To one he gave five bags of gold, to another two bags, and to another one bag, each according to his ability. Then he went on his journey. The man who had received five bags of gold went at once and put his money to work and gained five bags more. So also, the one with two bags of gold gained two more. But the man who had received one bag went off, dug a hole in the ground and hid his master's money.*
>
> *After a long time, the master of those servants returned and settled accounts with them. The man who had received five bags of gold brought the other five. 'Master,' he said, 'you entrusted me with five bags of gold. See, I have gained five more.' His master replied, 'Well done, good and faithful servant! You have been faithful with a few things; I will put you in charge of many things. Come and share your master's happiness!'*
>
> *The man with two bags of gold also came. 'Master,' he said, 'you entrusted me with two bags of gold; see, I have*

gained two more.' His master replied, 'Well done, good and faithful servant! You have been faithful with a few things; I will put you in charge of many things. Come and share your master's happiness!'"

Matthew 25:14- NIV

We know what happens to the third servant. He buried his talent and the master gets furious with him. He called him lazy and said he could have shown some effort by at least giving the talent to the bank so the talent could gain interest.

This applies to ministers for both the ministry and the minister themselves. We have been called into ministry and building it is determined by how we use the talents given to us while we wait for the master to return. Be faithful and diligent with your talent. God will multiply—every time.

BUILD A BUDGET

You must decide how much you are willing to spend when hosting your own service or another ministry. When you are starting out, you will only have personal resources. You have the option of credit cards or getting a loan from the bank, but start smart. Start where you can, without the use of credit or getting a loan.

When you start out, start with the lowest possible costs. I will share with you how I hosted my first seminar for people interested in building their own ministry with a budget that was like mine.

The event was from 10:00 am to 3:00 pm. Included with their event registration they received a book, a workbook and a catered lunch. Each desk had a bottle of water and an ink pen. When those attending arrived, the room was set up, music was playing and I had a friend working the registration/check in table. The following is an overview of the approximate costs:

Facility Rental: $500 for conference room
Technical Support: $140 agreed rate of $20/hour for 7 hours
Supplies: $35 notebooks, pens, water, and coffee
Meals: $15/person
Clean Up Fee: $250
Total Expense Cost: $940

The total expense cost does not include the book I purchased for each person I hoped would attend. I bought a case of books and paid $17/book + cost of shipping the case.

Books: $850

Without including the cost of the book, to break even on this event, I needed 20 people to register at a minimum of $47. Here's the thing: you can't do what I did and leave out any costs when you are figuring out your break-even point.

The first time I hosted this event, I charged $79. I had thirteen people register, two friends attend for moral (and technical) support, and I also had two guests attending who helped with set up and serving the food.

My actual event expenses (with books purchased): $1790
Income from registration (less processing fees): $962
Final reconciliation: -$828

I ended the day $828 upside down! Learn from my mistakes so your events will always be profitable. How could I prepare for my next event when I needed to create a payment plan for the last one?

This was a harsh and expensive learning curve. I knew that people would want to attend this event. I am an expert planner and advisor, but actual attendance did not meet my expectation. At the end of the day, I had to create a plan to get this event off the ground and build from a better foundation.

Whether it is for a free event or paid registration, the word "registration" can be an irritant to those who you had hoped would come to your event. For others, registration will not bother them because they perceive the value of what you are doing. Charging registration will give you an estimated attendance count, also called head count, for the service. It will help you determine and plan your budget as the event gets closer. Another benefit, is it gives you the start-up funds for securing the location, paying for additional advertising, or ordering the catering. It is what you can start with, but it could also be the entire supply for the budget.

I remember we were at an amazing event in Colorado. We arrived to set up the bookstore to see that the event was more over the top than what we were informed it would be. I mean that in the best possible way! We walked in to the foyer of the church, round-tables with beautiful linens and table decorations were set. A full coffee and tea bar was set up with snacks and desserts around it. It was the first night of the two-day event and the ministry who organized the event hired servers to restock the catered desserts. The next day was two services with a catered luncheon during the afternoon break. The tables had new table decorations, different flowers, fresh linens and ten people serving plated food to the guests. It was a three-course meal and it was superb! This event had a $25 registration and all I could think was there is no way they are going to break even.

As horrible as this sounds, it was true! I asked the church coordinator (who was overseeing the rental of the church building and coordinating with the guest ministry hosting our ministry), "How can they do this with a $25 registration? The set up last night would have been more than that per person. They did a great job of giving way more than what they charged for, but how can they do something like this and be able to host another ministry?"

The church coordinator said, "They host events like this all the time. They have a small registration cost so they know how many guests to plan for; they have always exceeded the value versus the price per person cost that they charge. It's just who they are … plus, her husband owns a big company and the business gives to support the ministry."

It made sense that the ministry was partnering with another organization. I love that it was a husband's enjoyment and blessings from his work that gave the ministry the opportunity to do more, give more, and bless more, to its supporters. I hope that more ministries can create partnerships on this level. Not just to have more over the top luncheons or conferences, but to truly partner with a ministry and increase its generosity in its outreach and ministry efforts would be creating Kingdom impact on an even greater scale!

ORGANIZE AND CREATE A MINISTRY SERVICE OR CONFERENCE

1. Ask God for a message

    a. He may inspire you through what you're reading in Bible

    b. Prayer requests or needs from those coming to your ministry

    c. Share your passion, anointing, or gifting

2. Create a theme

    a. Themes are like the slogan for the event

    b. It can be as short as one word

    c. It should be a phrase but not necessarily a complete sentence

    d. If it is too long, it will take up a lot of space on any advertising and social media postings

    e. If it is too long, people will have a hard time remembering what it is or hard to follow

    f. A carefully crafted theme will make it easier to create the advertising elements

    g. The theme should identify the takeaway for those who are attending

3. Consider your options to partner with other ministries

    a. Communicate expectations with
        the partnering ministry

        i.   Responsibilities: advertising, financing,
             and leading the service

        ii. Who will contact speakers, the venue
             or church, and recruit volunteers?

        iii. Delegate the work load and share the experience

    b. Identify the goal or purpose of the ministry
        event and agree that working together or
        collaborating efforts are a good idea

    c. Create the budget together, share expenses
        as co-sponsors to the event

4. Create or outline your budget

    a. Decide what you will and will not pay for

    b. Identify what is necessary and what
        is not necessary for the event

    c. Create an event budget

        i.   If the event has a co-sponsor, discuss a plan
             of action before spending or over spending

        ii. Plan how over spending is discussed and paid for

        iii. Discuss how expenses are covered and
             reimbursed to each sponsoring ministry

MONEY SAVER TIP

 It is much easier to talk about the money that will be spent versus money that has been spent without an agreement made. Money can be one of the toughest or most awkward conversations you can have, but having the conversation can prevent severe damage or complete destruction to the relationship.

Also, when you negotiate to cater food, rent a ballroom, or book a speaker, your ministry event needs to be a good steward and find a good deal. When you negotiate a contract or agree to a purchase, the seller needs to provide for their families or employees just as much as you do. When you convince people to do something for free or give you a 50% lower cost than what it should be, do not be surprised if the quality of their service is sacrificed to match the lower price. In the end, do not wish you had paid more to get a better service. The saying, "you get what you pay for" will always be true.

> d.   Start with known costs
>
>> i.   rental fee (venue, church, conference center, hotel ballroom)
>>
>> ii.   renter's insurance for the event location
>>
>> iii.   sound technician
>>
>> iv.   staff/volunteers
>>
>> v.   childcare
>>
>>> ◉   husbands and wives should not work or volunteer in the same classroom

- ◉ childcare applicant should submit a resume or application with a church or business recommendation

- ◉ background checks should always be used before a childcare applicant is accepted

- ◉ rental space for childcare

  - » snacks
  - » food allergy awareness

vi. food

vii. water

viii. advertising (online or printed)

- ◉ advertising created

  - » by graphic designer
  - » using smart phone applications

- ◉ printing

  - » vistaprint.com
  - » gotprint.com
  - » 4imprint.com

ix. resources – books, teachings, products, etc.

x. worship team members

- ◉ musicians –

  - » paid or volunteers (live music)
  - » recorded music

       xi. clean-up crew (if not included in rental fee)

      xii. ministry/guest speaker honorarium

     xiii. ministry/guest speaker transportation, whether by airplane or car

     xiv. ministry/guest speaker hotel accommodations

      xv. ministry/guest speaker travel with spouse or assistant

- meals

- transportation

- accommodations

  e. Create a margin for the unknown costs or incidentals

       i. 15% buffer or margin above spending limit

      ii. caterer tip

     iii. delivery fee

     iv. set up fee or non-refundable deposit

Starting with known expenses, you can create a formula to figure out how many people you need to have in the room. How many people need to register? What needs to be received in the offering to pay for the event? How much will come out of your pocket or savings to cover what has been spent?

CREATE AN ORDER OF SERVICE

This is creating a service flow, service schedule, or an outline for service. It marks the start and the end of the service, with all the details that go in the middle. It can list from the time staff or team members arrive to what time the doors are locked and the building is secured. A schedule for me would look something like this:

Evening Service Schedule Template

> 6:00 pm – Doors and Bookstore Open
>
> 6:30 pm – Childcare Opens
>
> 6:55 pm – 5 Minute Countdown and Live Streaming Begins
>
> 7:00 pm – Worship Team Starts Service
>
> 7:30 pm – Prayer
>
> 7:35 pm – Announcements, Offering and Upcoming Events
>
> Offering Song: _____
>
> + Transition to Introduce Guest Speaker
>
> 8:05 pm – Guest Speaker/Minister
>
> 9:15 pm – Guest Speaker Pray/Hosting Ministry Pray and Dismiss
>
> 9:30 pm – Childcare Closes
>
> 10:00 pm – Bookstore Closes
>
> 10:30 pm – Building Secured/Security Walk Through
>
> 10:40 pm – Light Out, Alarm On

It doesn't always stay on time. Actually, it never stays on time, but it is always good. A schedule is made for every service, every conference, and every event. Weeks before a conference date arrives, ministers that I help to host, have emailed or called requesting a service outline or schedule. They want to know what is planned. I have also helped to facilitate rentals of our conference center and guest speakers have asked me for an order of events sheet or outline. Unfortunately, during facility rentals, I have had to let people know that I do not know what the plan is because one had not been made.

Having an agenda or a plan for the service does not prevent the Holy Spirit from moving. It does not constrain Him to only move as I allow. Even recently, praise and worship was so powerful, I could not speak. I couldn't stop smiling and had this giggle that can only be explained as the joy of the Lord. I did not want the worship to stop and I couldn't pull myself together to transition the service from worship to the Word. I couldn't gather my thoughts to introduce the speaker. I managed to say, "Tonight, you get to transition yourselves to your seats. Please welcome Joan Hunter to the platform." It was an amazing night. The Holy Spirit moved, the anointing was so strong and I didn't let the planned schedule get completely lost. The timing was off and some of the details got missed, but the outcome from the time of ministry still happened as planned.

People received prayer and healing. We saw miracles happen, restoration, and oppression lifted. The ministry outcome was to see people encounter the love of God through, praise, worship, healing, deliverance and hear the Word of God.

As far as the schedule above, as you create and make an order of service, allow reasonable amounts of time for each part of the ministry service. After the service, compare the allotted time to the actual time and then plan your next service with applying an updated time frame. Let your worship team know how much time you want to have for worship. You can also let them know what you'll be teaching on (before the day of the service) and see if they can arrange the song list to flow into your message. When you take the time to create a service plan, you will find that your stress level or reliance on remembering what is supposed to happen next is not as necessary. You will be free to enjoy more of what is happening in the service versus trying to communicate what you want to your team to do in the middle of the service.

I make five to eight copies of the schedule. Each guest speaker gets a copy, a few team members get a copy, the sound booth has two copies and then I keep a copy. This way, everyone who is responsible for specific details for the service, know the plan and get the plan in motion as soon as the doors open.

OFFERING ETIQUETTE AND ACCOUNTABILITY

A financial offering is an amount of money that is between those attending and God alone. You can encourage people to give and share with them what giving to your ministry accomplishes. You can share the mission in motion or share Biblical teachings on giving. It is always up to you present the opportunity to give, but it is God and God alone that should tell them what to give.

People attending a ministry event will not be inspired to give if you receive or take an offering to "cover expenses." To me, that is like hosting a dinner party and while your guests are eating, you tell them how much their dinner cost. You invited them to dinner.

You made the dinner plans and added the dessert. If you are in over your head, you got there on your own. It is not the responsibility of your guests to reimburse you.

When the offering is received, collected and counted, remember that it is God's money. When the offering is being counted, always have two people in the room. Have a tally sheet or form to be completed that will have a place for a total cash, total checks, total credit card donations, then a place for a grand total. Regardless of the amount, declare that every offering is a good offering. Pray and bless every offering; people are giving to God in expectation of the harvest and with expectation that you will be a good steward of that gift as well.

AVOID UNNECESSARY SPENDING

1. Start with one service or a one day conference.

    a. Build your experience.

        i.   What did you like or didn't like about the service(s)?

        ii. What worked?

        iii. What didn't work?

        iv. Gain and increase participation and attendance.

2. Expenses for a multi-day event can multiply the cost for the event.

3. Meal planning tips:

        i.   Serve tea and water to drink.

ii. Sodas can increase your food bill without increasing the value of the meal.

iii. Cater with restaurants that can stay within your price per person.

» Recruiting help with meal preparation and serving, you could lower your cost per person.

» "Pot Luck Dinner" or "Covered Dish"- Individuals prepare and bring food as part of their contribution to the ministry event.

PREVENT HIDDEN COSTS FROM SHOWING UP

When you are creating your budget, build into your plan 15% cushion. For example, if you do not want to spend more than $1000, then your total event cost should be maxed out at $850. If you plan to spend $850 and end up spending $1000, you are still within your budget. If you budget for $1000 and spend $1150, you have over extended your budget by $150. This may not seem like a big deal; $150 is not a huge amount of money, but do you have it? Did your event sponsor or ministry partner agree to pay $150 more before the overage was spent?

Let's look at this with another set of numbers. What if your max event budget was $50,000? For $50,000, you're hosting a four-day ministry conference, at a hotel and flying in two guest speakers. Your budget including a 15% cushion is $42,500. If you go over the max budget, you will have spent $7,500 more than what you planned. I used two figures for this example, but the concept of overspending on any level can create a deficit and ministries cannot grow or be sustainable if they are always operating at a deficit. If you continue to spend more than what comes in you will stop operating and your ministry will no longer be sustainable.

STAFF YOUR SERVICE OR MINISTRY EVENT WISELY

As you are building your ministry, you will be the primary contributor and its biggest supporter. Most likely, you will host your first event with your strength and combined efforts with your spouse, family or closest friends. That is, if they are interested in what your ministry is doing. For some, their initial ministry events will be completed with God and their personal tenacity. They will build and grow with those efforts until they develop a team that love what the ministry has done for them. Once you have hired staff members, you will need to include them in the cost of your event. Plan for your team and for their participation in your ministry event while keeping in mind, staff hours are longer than the length of the service. They should be required to be there before and after the scheduled service time.

I prefer for our staff to arrive ninety minutes before a scheduled service. In some cases, they are there even earlier than that. The doors open an hour before the service starts and I want our staff ready and in position to welcome volunteers and guests. The worship team usually arrives three to four hours before the service starts. They set up their instruments, practice the songs for worship, and they need to be completed with sound check thirty minutes before the service starts. This is not always the case, but it is something that we aim for. Having the team arrive early reduces the opportunity for traffic to prevent someone from arriving in time to set up and practice.

HOW TO INVITE A GUEST SPEAKER TO YOUR MINISTRY

If you are inviting a friend to minister, then your invitation can be less formal. A word of warning, take care of your friends and honor them as you would any minister. In fact, you should go above and beyond for your friends. Exceed their expectations and never take advantage of them or their ministry. Never use them for your personal gain or leveraging your ministry. Before you ministered together, you were friends and you do not want to let something that is supposed to glorify God be the reason you are no longer friends. This applies to family members in ministry as well. Do not treat them like they are less valuable to what your ministry is doing because they are related to you. Ministries do not need drama from family or friends getting in the way of people's purpose or destiny.

Take care of your friends and honor them as you would any minister.

An informal invitation can start as a phone call or text message, but every invitation should always have a formal invitation sent whether a letter or email. Conversations get forgotten, communication on a cell phone could have been spotty, and a text message can convey the wrong tone.

Always honor your potential guests. Take the time to write a formal invitation and outline the conversation and any agreements that were made. Over-communicate and answer any questions your guest may have. A well written invitation answers questions before they are even asked.

Here are key things to include in your invitation:

1. Date

2. Location

3. Theme or Event Title/Purpose

4. Service Times

   a. Specifically list the service time that they will be speaking.

   b. How long they should teach and minister?

   c. Can they mention or recommend a ministry resource like a book or teaching?

   d. Let them know if other speakers are invited and attending.

5. Registration Cost (if any)

6. Accommodations

   a. Include hotel, travel, and transportation

   b. What costs you will cover or reimburse for them?

   c. Food – Have meal plans and schedule ready; ask about food allergies or special diet requests.

7. Book Store

  a. Book table, table cloth and volunteer provided

  b. Volunteer can provide the following: set up, inventory products upon arrival and departure and sell resources for them

8. Honorarium/Offering

  a. A financial gift for their ministry services

  b. Split of registration income or offering

9. Expectations should be made clear so that both ministries desire the same outcome for the ministry service.

10. Contact person, whether it is you or your assistant, who can they list on their website for this ministry event?

11. Contact person, whether it is you or your assistant, who do they contact if they have questions about coordinating the ministry service?

This may seem overwhelming, but the clearer you can make the conversation or expectations, the easier the service will be. I have seen events where the hosting ministry did not supply a lot of information: things like registration was charged, registration was cancelled due to a lack of support, event themes changed right before the date of the event arrived, speakers cancelled at the last minute, and moving/changing locations close to the date of the event. Avoid as much last minute changes as you possibly can. Every single one of these things can have a major negative impact on the ministry service. Big changes can negatively affect the attendance, the accuracy of the advertising, and the overall outcome of the event. It creates inconsistency and can cause a loss of interest in your ministry if it happens too often.

HOW TO GET AND RESPOND TO INVITATIONS TO MINISTER

1. Make yourself available. Make time in your schedule to say yes to invitations that have come from friends in ministry or people willing to share their platform with you.

2. Prepare a Series of Messages

   a. 5 minutes

   b. 15-20 minutes

   c. 45 minutes

   d. 60 minutes

3. Create a digital portfolio

   a. Picture of you, headshot or a quality picture of you ministering

      i. Not blurry, pixilated or a "selfie" from your cell phone

      ii. Invest money or barter with a friend to get a professional picture taken

      iii. Good lighting

      iv.   Avoid a distracting background

      v.   Avoid wearing solid white on camera

  b.   Short and intentional biography

  c.   Contact information

      i.   Ministry name, website and phone number

      ii.   Social media links

  d.   Letters of recommendation from previous hosts or ministry recommendations

      i.   They don't need to be long

      ii.   They need to validate your ability to minister or do what you say you can do

Every invitation should be received with honor and gratitude. Then it should be prayerfully considered. An invitation does not always mean a that a date is going to get booked and go on your calendar. There are several factors to weigh in addition to giving God the ability to speak to you and say "Go" or "Don't Go."

Here are some questions to ask yourself before saying yes or no to an invitation:

- God, do you want me to go?

- Do I fundamentally agree with their understanding and application of Biblical principles?

- Do our ministries believe and teach in agreement with each other and with God?

- Do I know them or their reputation as a hosting ministry?

- Do I know anyone that has been hosted by them before?

  - Would they return and minister there again? How were they treated?

- Does the invitation explain how I will get to the service?

- What arrangements are being considered?

- Am I responsible for covering my own expenses?

- What do they expect of me (or from me) during the ministry time?

PREPARE YOUR MESSAGE

Keep in mind how much time you have been asked to share. When you go outside of the requested ministry time, this is something that your hosts will keep in mind when they are considering hosting you again. I have been at church, listening to a guest speaker, and have felt like I was trapped. The following Sunday, the pastor apologized for how long the service went and insisted that the guest speaker would probably never speak there again. As of the writing of this book, it has been more than ten years and I am confident that the guest speaker was never invited back to the church I was attending.

Keep in mind those that are attending with you. Once a message has five points made, your audience could begin to wonder how many more points are there? Are you going to let us out before 2:00 pm on this beautiful Sunday? Are you going to make the volunteers in the nursery resent you for going over while they have hungry and crying babies?

Steven Covey in *Seven Habits of Highly Effective People*, made the point: "Begin with the end in mind." For most, this quote is about making a profit or being more productive. I want you to think about the end of your moment of ministry with your audience. Yes, God is listening to you and cheering you on, but I want you to think about those who will talk about you when you are done. Think about what you want them to think, feel and do, when you are done ministering. If you consider that in your plans and message material, you will set your aim to make them think, feel and do something with the message you just shared with them.

TEACHING OR MINISTRY NOTES

Create notes with scripture references, stories you want to share and have them in a form of an outline. A mentor of mine has always said, "Every story should have a point and every point should have a story." Apply this to a ministry service, if you start with a theme, search out scriptures and then create life application, you are doing just about what he said to do.

Select a scripture, share a story of how it applies to you or the meaning of it. In the follow up, give another example through sharing a story, then relate it to scripture. If your message is five stories and two illustrations, but you do not include scripture, then how are you ministering? Don't get me wrong, but your ministry should always reflect what God is doing in your life or what He has done in your life. It cannot be built or sustained on what you have done for God alone. The ministry is about expanding His Kingdom, not our own.

Have fun with your outline and make it easy to follow. Handwritten notes are a great start to organizing your message. You can also start by creating a document on your computer. Before you arrive at the service to minister, I recommend typing and printing out your notes. If you have a second person going with you, let them have a copy of your notes as well. This is for a few reasons:

- If you are nervous or stumbling through handwritten notes, you run the risk of not being able to read your outline.

- Having them printed before you arrive on location, shows that you are prepared and ready to minister.

- If you have a second copy available, and you spill coffee or water on your copy, you already have a backup ready to go.

If your notes are in a document, you can also create your outline to be easy to follow. I use bolded text to emphasis the words in a scripture or story. I use a larger font size than I write or would normally type with; making it easy to read or follow at a glance.

I was recently at a conference and I attended to see the way another group was ministering, to hear the ministers and receive from their revelation and life experiences. One of the speakers was adorable in their presentation. They had a yellow note pad with their handwritten notes and they went from line to line with their message. It was inspiring and passionate. They shared great stories and gave God glory for their salvation experience and all that started in that one moment. It almost moved me to tears.

Another speaker got up and they were just as prepared. They had pages of notes, an illustration, and a powerful prayer. Even though the message was good, I found that I was distracted by the lack of organization in the notes. The message overall encouraged me to praise God in all circumstances, but nothing really stood out to me as far as revelation or content and I can tell you why. As I was listening, the speaker was fumbling through several pages (of different sizes and colors) of notes for the next thing to say. Then, when they spoke, it was hard to follow and it made me nervous.

I could have been the only person to notice what was happening and I was probably the only one who got nervous because of it. I was nervous for my friend. I wanted them to a give a good, strong message, but I felt like if they could have streamlined their message to make it flow better, they would have been less flustered and I wouldn't have gotten nervous. I did not tell them how I felt or what I thought of the message. If they wanted my opinion or to acknowledge that I probably had an opinion to give, they would have asked me for it. Because they didn't, I did not comment or give advice as to what they could have done to make it better.

I hope for the best and only want the best for people. I want to see them succeed and truly do what God has called them to do. This is a big reason why I would take the time and resources necessary to help communicate the content in this book. When you prepare and even over-prepare, I believe that God honors that and He multiplies our efforts. I believe that we can submit our outline or message to Him and He will help us remove or ignore what is not needed and add what is beneficial and prophetic to convey His heart to His people.

If and when you do what I did, and think about the way a speaker could have done something better, be nice and keep your thoughts to yourself. Unless they share their journey with you, you will never know how hard it was for them to share their message. Plus, keep in mind, the fear of public speaking is real and it prevents people from picking up a microphone or standing on a platform. In fact, 7% of the people in the United States, which is about 27 million people, have a fear of public speaking.[1]

Also, unless you are telling someone that they did a great job and how much it blessed you, do not give unsolicited constructive criticism. If they did not ask you for your opinion, then do not make it a priority to share it with them. This is a seed sown with a possible lifetime harvest you do not want to reap.

SELF-PRESENTATION AND MINISTRY PRESERVATION

Dr. Clarice Fluitt is one of my favorite mentors. During a coaching call with her she said, "Melody, I love you, but you need to make sure your mess doesn't take away from your message." I thought, *What does she mean by that?*

"Don't worry," she went on and explained the principle of dressing for the job you want, not the job you have. Shortly before this call with Dr. Clarice, another friend and mentor, Wendy K. Walters said, "You know Melody, to do what you want to do, you are going to have to dress differently. This means, that you don't get to get on the platform again wearing a t-shirt, jeans and tennis shoes. You need to dress like an expert. Dress for the platform you desire to be speaking on."

At that, it was perfectly clear. I needed to invest in a different wardrobe than what I was used to. Some days are long days and some conferences go on for four or five days. That is a lot of dressing up, perfect make up and good hair days that get to be back-to-back. By the end of day two or sometimes day three, my feet are ready for tennis shoes and I would much rather wear jeans with my hair tied up, but I don't do that. I hear the voice of wisdom in the form of Dr. Clarice or Wendy's voice, and I pull myself together and get my mess out of the way of my message.

Since adjusting my clothing and adjusting my style, I have gotten more positive feedback from people than I ever have before. They love the message more, the inspiration is stronger, the delivery is more polished and invitations to speak or coach clients has increased. I was willing to listen to feedback that was directly connected to a result I wanted. I strive to always be polished and prepared as a teacher or minister. I wanted to increase ministry invitations and increase my coaching clients. Changing the way I dressed, improved the quality of the ministry presentation and created ministry preservation. Depending on your desired outcome for building or sustaining your ministry, you may have to change the way you dress or the style of your delivery.

Keep in mind, God has called and equipped you with His plans and purpose, so with every feedback or constructive criticism you receive, take it to God. Ask Him to show the truth of what was said. Ignore how it was said or if it was said just to hurt or distract you. Qualify the voices that you allow to speak to the direction of your delivery. This is a subject for your inner circle, board members, elders, or family/friends who want the best for you, who can speak to and you should be able to hear their heart for you and know that their intent is not to hurt or destroy you. I'm sure for both Dr. Clarice and for Wendy, that long before they said something about my jeans, they had thought about it. I know that they waited until their relationship with me was stronger and their intent for me as a speaker was clear. You may not have the opportunity to share your voice or concerns for someone in ministry, but before you share your opinion, build and strengthen your relationship with them, so that if the opportunity is presented, the relationship will be strong enough to carry the weight of your opinion.

TURN YOUR MESSAGES INTO MINISTRY RESOURCES

My first book is a collaboration of six different ministry messages that the Holy Spirit gave me, as well as, life application and personal experiences in line with the title *While You Are Waiting: How to Make the Most of Where You Are*. The live messages are available on CDs, DVDs, and in conference sets.

When you are developing resources, you are creating a stream of income for you and for your ministry. How things are paid for and in agreement with your ministry board or elders, you can arrange payment, reimbursement and royalties for products written, recorded and sold. In the process, always protect yourself and your ministry. Be sure that the product you have made available is your content or context, and make sure when you release a "new product" it is new and not just a summary or updated version of a previous release. If it is the updated, revised or summary of something else, then say so. Make it clear for those who support your ministry that

new package of an old product. If you fail
ecline in your sales, as well as, supporters.

ource you make available, keep the standard
uncompromised. Protect the quality of the
he quantity of messages available. Protect
esentation. Make the resource value more
concern for profit from it. Create packages,
e specials while you are at an event and give
tners and volunteers discounted rates to say
y do for your ministry.

ll need multiple streams of income in order to
owth. Plan now for the streams to form from
n ministry. Write books, go on speaking tours,
most importantly, do what God has called you
y. Be the change agent, hope pusher, kingdom
s made you to be!

tps://magneticspeaking.com/7-unbelievable-
ar-of-public-speaking-statistics/.

Planning is bringing your
into the present so that you
something about it now.

A

they are not buying the
to do so, you will see a

Overall, with every res
of excellence high and
message more than t
the packaging and p
important than the
bundles or conferenc
your supporters, pa
thank you for all the

Your ministry wi
build or sustain g
your best efforts i
host conferences;
to do in ministr
expander God ha

future
can do

an Lakein

r is a coach who knows how to make people
! With wisdom beyond her years, Melody
. She leads willing participants down the path
ish their mission, how to discover and map
d plan, and how to reach for the fulfillment of
r their life. She will show you how to LIVE your

ll Team Certified speaker and coach, Melody
leadership development and reaching personal
cused pursuit of this passion is evident in every
l coaching opportunity.

ing for life changing inspiration that sparks change
ight for overcoming obstacles, Melody Barker is
e appointment!

Attitude is Adjustable. Purp
Everything is Poss

- Invite Melody to Speak

- Sign Up for Leadership & Persona
  Growth Training Events

- Engage Melody as Coach ... Get Pro

www.melodybarker.co